The Ethics of Undercover Policing

||| || | ||||||||| || ||| |||| |||
I0123751

Despite the media controversies surrounding high-profile cases of undercover policing, it is not always clear what ethical issues are at stake. Can undercover policing be justified? What are the ethical issues surrounding concealment and infiltration? What larger questions does undercover policing raise about the nature of policing and the legitimacy of coercive state action?

In this timely and clear account, Christopher Nathan explores these questions and more. He rejects the view that the consequences of undercover policing always justify the means, instead advancing an argument that through their actions people can make themselves morally liable to some forms of undercover policing. Drawing on several recent, high-profile case studies, Christopher Nathan argues for a new understanding of proportionality in undercover policing that takes account of innocent parties, vulnerable targets, and manipulation into wrongful action. He also defends a central role for the judiciary in the oversight of undercover policing.

Christopher Nathan is a research fellow in the Faculty of Politics and International Studies, University of Warwick, UK.

Routledge Focus on Philosophy

Routledge Focus on Philosophy is an exciting and innovative new series, capturing and disseminating some of the best and most exciting new research in philosophy in short book form. Peer reviewed and at a maximum of fifty thousand words shorter than the typical research monograph, *Routledge Focus on Philosophy* titles are available in both ebook and print on demand format. Tackling big topics in a digestible format the series opens up important philosophical research for a wider audience, and as such is invaluable reading for the scholar, researcher and student seeking to keep their finger on the pulse of the discipline. The series also reflects the growing interdisciplinarity within philosophy and will be of interest to those in related disciplines across the humanities and social sciences.

Honouring and Admiring the Immoral
An Ethical Guide
Alfred Archer and Benjamin Matheson

Newton's Third Rule and the Experimental Argument for Universal Gravity
Mary Domski

The Philosophy and Psychology of Commitment
John Michael

The Ethics of Undercover Policing
Christopher Nathan

For more information about this series, please visit: www.routledge.com/Routledge-Focus-on-Philosophy/book-series/RFP

The Ethics of Undercover Policing

Christopher Nathan

Routledge
Taylor & Francis Group

LONDON AND NEW YORK

First published 2022
by Routledge
4 Park Square, Milton Park, Abingdon, Oxon OX14 4RN

and by Routledge
605 Third Avenue, New York, NY 10158

Routledge is an imprint of the Taylor & Francis Group, an informa business

British Library Cataloguing-in-Publication Data
A catalogue record for this book is available from the British Library

Library of Congress Cataloging-in-Publication Data
A catalog record for this book has been requested

ISBN: 978-0-367-26458-1 (hbk)
ISBN: 978-1-032-27075-3 (pbk)
ISBN: 978-0-429-29344-3 (ebk)

DOI: 10.4324/9780429293443

Typeset in Times New Roman
by Apex CoVantage, LLC

Contents

Acknowledgements

I am very grateful to Matthew Clayton, Lisa Cockle, Antony Duff, Tim Grant, Kat Hadjimatheou, Keith Hyams, Simon McKay, Seumas Miller, Tom Sorell, Suzanne Uniacke and CAPPE, and audiences at Canberra, Manchester, Hong Kong, Oxford, UCL, and Warwick. I would also like to thank Elena Giroli of Creative Works and the Trencherfield Allotment Association. Special thanks, as ever, are due to Emily McTernan.

1 Undercover policing and the ideal

1 Context, outline, and goals

'"Lead us not into temptation", Judge Noonan warned. . . . But into temptation the Government has gone, ensnaring chroni-cally unemployed individuals from poverty-ridden areas in its fake drug stash-house robberies.' Thus begins the judgment of the 2014 case *U.S.* v. *Hudson, Whitfield & Dunlap*, an appeal by people who received long sentences for crimes committed in fictitious circumstances created by undercover agents for the Bureau of Alcohol, Tobacco, Firearms, and Explosives. In a con-troversy in the UK, undercover police formed relationships with activists (and their female acquaintances) in the groups that they infiltrated. One subject of this treatment stated years later in Par-liament:

> I met [the undercover officer Mark Kennedy] when I was 29, and he disappeared about three months before I was 35. It was the time when I wanted to have children, and for the last 18 months of our relationship he went to relationship counselling with me about the fact that I wanted children and he did not.[1]

These egregious cases illustrate the defining impact that undercover policing can have on people's lives. They also harbour complexity: how exactly should we account for the serious wrongs that were done? Can undercover policing be legitimate in principle, and if so, then what sort of governance structure would be most effective in ensuring its legitimacy?

DOI: 10.4324/9780429293443-1

More broadly, this book illustrates the importance of the normative status of the police and policing for those working in political
and legal theory. Other coercive state institutions like armies, property, and the law have existed for a long time and correspondingly
have received a great deal of attention from philosophers since the
ancients. Police, on the other hand, are relatively novel in human
history, especially in anything like their current form. They should
not be conceptualised as a simple extension of the law; it is well
established that both individually and as an institution, police hold
a significant amount of discretion in the exercise of their executive
powers,[2] and, as we will see, undercover policing is not an exception.
It is therefore important for those considering the nature of coercive
state power to understand what framework ought to govern these
police actions.

Undercover policing is increasingly being used.[3] This increase
is part of a larger policing trend towards greater reliance on surveillance and covert operations. According to one source, this rep-
resents a 'radical change to a traditional law enforcement model',
which hithertofore has been 'based on visibility and transparency'.[4]
Surveillance and covert practices, of course, have long existed.[5]
Undercover policing in particular has a bad press. In this book I ask,
what would an ideal undercover policing order look like? I reject
the view that undercover work is inherently at odds with the police
role, but I also reject the view that undercover work can be justified
by straightforwardly weighing its disvalue against its good consequences. Rather, some people can, through their actions, make themselves morally liable to intrusions and manipulations by the police,
while others – those who are innocent or uninvolved – are less liable
or not liable at all to such treatment. Although intuitive, this idea
is surprisingly absent in key ways from both the political debate
and governance structures relating to policing. Indeed, that absence
may partly explain some of the mistreatment of citizens by police
in recent decades. The book examines the liability idea through the
cleaner case of personal self-defence, bringing to bear the recent
sophisticated advances in the philosophical literature on that topic on
policing practice. In doing so, I argue for a new understanding of proportionality in undercover police work, one that takes due account
of innocent parties, vulnerable targets, disclosure, and manipulation into wrongful action. Further, the book uses this framework to

defend a central role for the judiciary in the oversight structure of undercover police, a role that is currently absent or heavily curtailed in most jurisdictions.

In this chapter, I examine the concept of undercover policing and the forms that it typically takes. I set out how it can be beneficial and then consider and reject some arguments against its use. In doing so, I set out the idealised theoretical stance of the book. The remainder of the text is divided as follows. Chapter 2 examines more closely the harms of undercover policing and considers and rejects several frameworks for thinking about the ethics in this area. In Chapters 3 and 4, I set out and defend my own position, the 'liability view', and Chapters 5 and 6 apply it to police manipulation and policy.[6]

2   The concept of undercover policing

Here is a definition. *Undercover policing involves the concealment from their targets of the identity of a police officer* as *an officer.*[7] This definition does not depend on the presence of manipulation. Although undercover policing is widely associated with efforts at manipulation, it need not involve such efforts, beyond the deception of people into believing that the officer is not an officer. Thus, some undercover police work does not involve an attempt to influence people's behaviour. Test buys of drugs may fall under this category, with the caveat that some test buys can involve a great deal of persuasive effort, and the more trivial caveat that, had the target not bought *this* contraband from *this* individual, she would have bought it from a *different* individual.[8] This definition focuses, rather, on the *sine qua non* of undercover work, which is the concealment from the public of the policing purposes of the state agent that they are dealing with.

Undercover policing will typically involve actions on the part of the officer that are aimed at obtaining either intelligence about or direct evidence of criminal activity. This is not a part of the earlier definition, however, since undercover policing that does not aspire to address criminal activity still *is* a form of undercover policing. Police may extend beyond their proper function, for example, in working on operations that are centrally aimed at subverting legitimate political groups.[9]

There are some edge cases of undercover policing that are not covered by the earlier definition, which renders it conceptually impossible for those state agents who are not enrolled in the police force to carry out undercover policing. But there may be cases in which we would want to say that state agents are acting *as* undercover police officers, even if they are not officially labelled as police officers and indeed would forego that title.[10] For example, local councils have used trained undercover inspectors to identify 'rogue traders' by making test purchases of fireworks, alcohol, and knives.[11] And we can imagine cases in which local council inspectors would also be deployed in positions of community power in order to identify those who illegitimately claim state benefits, or in which the undercover policing role is outsourced to the intelligence agencies rather than the police force. The point here is that we should not be beholden to the self-definitions that we are provided with by state institutions, but, rather, we should follow the function of what they do.

Sometimes, then, it will be useful to use an expansive, functional definition: *Undercover policing is the concealment of the policing function of a state agent.* This second definition has the advantage of also capturing those who carry out the role of undercover police officer without declaring themselves as such. Furthermore, there are some state agents who have a policing function that does not require them to interact with the public. Examples are those performing administrative roles within the police force, and those within the intelligence services who act as undercover agents focusing on domestic crime. Where the focus of our investigation is normative, as it is here, it is better to have a functional definition of our subject matter.

It is also worth pointing to the practice by some businesses of recruiting ex-undercover officers.[12] While such cases are not strictly instances of *state* spying, and are thereby not applications of police function, there may be cases in which the corporation that employs the individual is powerful enough to be, from a normative perspective, subject to the same kinds of considerations that I set out in this book. It is also possible for there to be non-state agents who are acting under contract or in some way under the control of the state, and thereby to be undercover officers for the purpose of analysis, even if, once again, they are not enrolled police officers.

A paradigm case of undercover policing is the fake 'fence', a business covertly run by police that aims at attracting purchases from those involved in criminal activity.[13] Another paradigm of undercover work involves the infiltration of an organisation. The infiltration will be carried out in an ongoing manner. Rather than terminating immediately on the apprehension of any criminal activity, the operation will continue with the goal of building a criminal case against those who are more central in the organisation. The activity being investigated may be serious crime involving weapons, drugs, fraud, trafficking, child sexual abuse, and terrorism. It is also used against political groups that aim at sabotage or violence.

A marginal case of the category of undercover policing might be a concealed speed trap. This does not involve the concealment of an individual's role as a state agent with a policing function, but it does involve the concealment of the presence of a policing function. And some of the principles governing the good governance of speed traps mirror those that apply to the good governance of undercover policing. People find it objectionable where speed traps are placed in ways that seems disproportionate. In the UK, traps can only be placed where there has been a fatality or serious injury. And people find the speed traps to be *pro tanto* more acceptable where they are not concealed. Something about the hidden functioning of this form of policing raises questions that need to be addressed. Traps can be placed in somewhat manipulative ways. For example, two can be placed close together so as to capture those who speed up immediately after passing through one.

Another close case to that of undercover policing is the informant, and especially the paid informant. Although not employed as a state agent in the way that a police officer is, a paid informant receives ongoing payments from police in exchange for information about an illicit organisation. Such payments can be significant and where they form the main part of a person's income, it seems that they will be cases that also fall within our functional definition of 'undercover police', since the policing function is effectively outsourced to them. That the agent lacks the formal training or employment contract should not remove them from the considerations of ethics and principles of governance that apply to undercover police. Some informants, however, *are* qualitatively different cases, especially those who are vulnerable. For the purposes of this text, it will be useful to consider the use of informants alongside the use of under-cover police, as the one is sometimes proposed as an alternative to the other.

3   Two kinds of undercover policing

For the purposes of making moral assessments, we can distinguish two paradigmatic kinds of undercover police work.[14] These are:

> *The Sting.* The use of undercover police officers to create an opportunity to commit a crime.
> *The Infiltration.* The placement of undercover police officers within a group or organisation.

The paradigmatic sting aims at an arrest for the action for which an opportunity is created. Stings range in sophistication from test buys at newsagents to fake gun businesses. Police can pretend to be a co-conspirator, a purchaser of goods, or a seller of goods. They can also pose as potential victims of crime. In each case, the path for a criminal act is facilitated by an undercover officer,[15] and evidence is thereby gathered for an arrest and prosecution. Although the paradigmatic sting aims at a prosecution, the police can make use of intelligence about criminal acts in other ways. The hope may be that the target will 'flip' and provide evidence or serve as an infor-mant. Furthermore, the publicising of the practice of stings may have the policy goal of creating a chilling effect.[16] For example, doubts among potential consumers about the veracity of offers of sales of weapons or images of child sexual abuse can be expected to inhibit the distribution of these products by disrupting the market.[17]

Stings can be targeted in a focused or a diffused way. A focused sting is deployed on the basis of prior intelligence, which itself can be gained through undercover work. For example, an investigation leads police to believe that a group is dealing in stolen goods, and police deploy an undercover officer who presents credible profitable opportunities. Stings have more diffused targeting, on the other hand, where they are based on no prior intelligence, or on intelligence that is speculative or is geographically based or otherwise linked to a particular sphere of action. For example, police may pose as tourists in a busy shopping area where it is known that pickpockets operate.

The kind of opportunity that is presented by a sting varies according to how actively the police officer alters the situation in which the targets would otherwise find themselves. A purely passive sting precisely mimics the kind of opportunity that the target would have had, with the only difference that an undercover police officer is providing it. There are numerous reasons why police may seek to make the opportunity less purely authentic.[18] Moving the location of a criminal opportunity may make it easier to obtain evidence or to protect undercover officers from possible harm. There are absolute costs and opportunity costs to authenticity: offering slightly above the market rate for stolen goods may clinch a deal that would otherwise have folded; leaving the wallets sticking out slightly further on decoy pickpocket victims makes it more likely that they will be victimised instead of tourists. Furthermore, encouraging undercover officers to create roles for themselves that fully meet the target's expectations may make it more likely that they will be placed in situations in which they must either commit criminal or otherwise undesirable acts, or risk undermining their cover.

Infiltration involves placing an undercover officer within a criminal organisation. Paradigmatically, in this role,

> the law enforcement officer divorces himself from his true persona. He doesn't carry any police credentials, and carries a gun only when the role he is playing calls for it. He lives at a UC residence, contacts his agency only through his handler (whom he sees infrequently), and has a wallet full of identification and credit cards (assuming his role would have these) in his UC identity. He may have a complete criminal history, credit report and other background data established in the UC persona.[19]

Infiltration can have one or more of several different purposes. It will likely involve direct gathering of evidence. But it can also have broader goals. It can seek *intelligence*, rather than merely evidence, looking to obtain an understanding of where investigations might next be targeted. It can have the goal of controlling or disrupting an organisation. There has long been a trend towards this kind of policing.[20] Infiltration may be used in order to address crimes that have already been committed, as where an undercover

officer befriends those suspected of serious crime. Infiltration paradigmatically involves an organisation, but individuals may also be
targeted.

As with stings, police activity may be more or less active. The
less active infiltration does not seek to affect the target's behaviour.
A passive infiltration can function like an 'ambulatory wiretap'.[21]
An officer gets a job at financial institution that is believed to be
involved in money laundering and use his position to gather written and spoken information about the organisation's workings. On
the other hand, active infiltration may involve obtaining information by deliberately affecting the behaviour of the targets, for example, through forming friendships and encouraging these friends to
work more closely with those at the centre of the target organisation. Undercover operations also become more active when they go
beyond the goal of information-gathering. This may occur through
preventive measures, such as sabotage of explosives that are to be
used by a terrorist group.

Infiltrations can – and often do – incorporate stings. Indeed,
infiltrations will typically be planned with an evidence-gathering
exercise leading to a prosecution. Alternatively, police may
decide that the value of further intelligence from continuing an
operation is not worth its costs and that prosecutions should be
sought against members of the target organisation. Activity that
has taken place during the infiltration may thus be grounds for a
prosecution.

4   Benefits

It is difficult to sustain the position that undercover policing cannot sometimes yield real benefits that relate to the normal range
of functions of policing. For example, Operation Chandler was an
international cooperation between police agencies that successfully
infiltrated and brought down a large online group that commissioned
child abuse and distributed the images.[22] The operation worked by
studying the online personas of several known members, arresting
them, and having undercover officers mimic them in chatrooms so
as to gain more knowledge of the ring's other members. The ring
was ultimately brought down after a series of arrests worldwide,
and prosecutions were built upon the evidence that was gathered by

the online undercover officers. The Child Exploitation and Online Protection Centre (CEOP) describes the case as follows:

In April 2006, 27-year-old Timothy David Martyn Cox started the chatroom 'Kids The Light Of Our Lives'. From the large farmhouse in Buxhall, Suffolk which he shared with his parents and sister, Cox spent hours each day in his bedroom orchestrating the site. This allowed like-minded paedophiles to share images and videos of child sex abuse and plans for abusing victims ranging from the age of babies to young teens. Soon the site had attracted more than 700 users from all over the world, 200 of them in the UK. Cox used the name 'I*Do*It' when trading images, some of which were shocking pictures of children being subjected to sadistic abuse. In August 2006, Canadian members of the Virtual Global Taskforce (VGT) passed intelligence about Cox's network to the Child Exploitation and Online Protection (CEOP) Centre, who carried out a period of covert surveillance. Police arrested Cox on 28th September 2006, allowing them to spend 10 days posing as him online in order to gather further information about the site's users and the children they were abusing. Meanwhile, they found 75,960 indecent images of children on Cox's computer, and evidence he had supplied 11,491 images to other site users. Following Cox's removal as host and the closure of the site, 33-year-old Gordon Mackintosh from Hertfordshire, who went by the usernames 'silentblackheart' and 'lust4skoolgurls', tried to have the room reinstated and was arrested on 9th January 2007. On his PC were 5,167 indecent images of children and 392 indecent movie files. Worldwide, the investigation into the users of 'Kids The Light Of Our Lives' has led to the safeguarding of more than 40 children from abuse or positions of harm.[23]

Could the same benefit – the cessation of the ring's activities, and the prosecution of its central members – have been achieved without the use of undercover policing? It seems doubtful. The core participants used encryption and other security precautions in order to protect themselves. Only by using socially manipulative methods does it seem technically possible for the central members of the group to have given up information that would have permitted police to locate them physically.

Such operations also have a preventive benefit. They have a welcome chilling effect upon the kinds of activities that they seek to prevent. The dark side of the online world is replete with suspicion about the identity of its members. By demonstrating that they can act undercover, police can be expected to sow distrust among those who are seeking to cooperate on criminal matters. Overcoming such distrust is not impossible, but it is costly, in the dark web taking the form of closed groups with strict entry criteria, slower communication architecture, and careful attention to anonymity measures. The point, of course, applies offline as well as online. Even in the context of electronic surveillance, those who are seeking, for example, to fund a trafficking and terrorism group would be rational to take measures to ensure that none of its members is a police officer, revealing its workings only to those who have built up a relationship of trust with existing core members. Undercover operations thereby slow down wrongful activity even where that activity is not infiltrated, and may indeed do so to the extent that absent the suspicion it sows, a significant degree of seriously criminal activity is prevented altogether.[24]

The general benefits of the undercover tactic will fall under the headings concerned with the general purposes of policing. Most prominently, these are greater prevention of crimes, harms, and rights violations, and greater facilitation of the criminal justice system.[25]

5   Against police as they are

Having looked at undercover policing and its potential benefits, let us consider the question of justification. Undercover policing involves activities that are, on the face of things, serious wrongs. It involves agents of the state deliberately deceiving and manipulating citizens and intruding upon their private lives. It can cause direct psychological harms to those who are targeted, ranging from a sense of broken trust to ongoing trauma. It can also harm people in materially redirecting their lives in ways that are not best for them and that they would not choose. Aside from effects on those targeted, it also can have deleterious effects on the officers who carry out the work, on innocent third parties, and on public trust in and therefore the effective functioning of the criminal justice system. The task in this book, then, is to set out a framework that describes when and how the practice is justified.

The right place to start is with the possibility that undercover work is never justified. The advantage of attending to the sceptical possibility is that if it is true, then we will have landed upon an important result, while if it is ultimately rejected, we will be able to proceed on a firmer footing, reaching for justifications of precise elements of the practice by depending not upon the way things are done now, but on an understanding of the way things ought to be done. The police are such a new institution, by historical standards, that there is especially strong reason to seek to rest our arguments on principles rather than existing practices, which in the case of policing have undergone less of the scrutiny of time than other coercive state institutions.

There are two broad versions of the argument that all or a large part of undercover policing is unjustified *tout court*. The first argument is that undercover policing is unjustified because it is an element of policing, and the police themselves are unjustified. The second is that undercover policing is inconsistent with the proper functions of policing and is therefore an incoherent practice on its own terms. In the context of the ongoing scandals around policing, one hears allusions to both arguments, and indeed will often hear them both together. Consider, first, objections to police forces as a whole:

> Any real agenda for police reform must replace police with empowered communities working to solve their own problems. . . . Policing will never be a just or effective tool for community empowerment, much less racial justice. . . . We don't need empty police reforms; we need a robust democracy that gives people the capacity to demand of their government and themselves.[26]

The functioning of policing de facto reflects wider injustices, and in the absence of a thoroughly uprooted and reimagined institution, the power and discretion possessed by individual police officers will only reflect those wider injustices. This is a serious objection to policing as a whole.[27] Vitale's objection to police reform in particular is that the background mission of the police undermines efforts at reform:

> As long as the basic mission of police remains unchanged, none of these reforms will be achievable. There is no technocratic fix. Even if we could somehow implement these changes, they would be ignored, resisted, and overturned – because the institutional imperatives of the politically motivated wars on drugs, disorder, crime, etc., would win out.[28]

It may be the case that these institutional imperatives (as well as the surrounding background injustices) are so entrenched that it is impossible for us to get to anything approaching an ideal institution within, say, the next century. Such an argument may point to evidence of systematic prejudice and abuse of power, such as patterns of police brutality or the practice of using dead children's identities as a part of undercover officer's background stories,[29] and urge that such outcomes are a consequence of social forces that exist beyond the police.

I proceed here, nonetheless, with the hope that an understanding of the principles that would make policing ultimately justified can aid progress both in improving the background political mission of policing and in informing particular reforms. I will assume that we are working with an idealised police force; that there are no systematic abuses of power, and that the laws that the police are tasked to uphold are more or less just.

There is some danger that doing ideal theory at this level has the rhetorical implication that police forces are much closer to the ideal than they are, and that reform is much more straightforward than it is. We should be clear: police forces are not ideal. The value of doing theory in an imagined world in which systematic explicit and implicit prejudices and overreach do not exist is that it gives us a stronger sense of what would be right and in what direction to travel. Of course, this does not deal with the other half of the abolitionist objection, namely, that ideal theorising carries an unwarranted insinuation that we might *get* to the ideal. In response to this, even unreachable ideals can be crucially motivating in seeking justice, especially ideals that are purported to be unreachable *because* of wider injustices.[30]

A further objection holds that the kind of ideal theorising carried out here is an unhelpful sort. It is not a pure ideal world that I assume. While assuming away systematic prejudice and overreach within the police force, I do not assume away crime, and indeed at several points I positively assume the existence of systematic or organised crime, since that is the kind of crime that undercover policing is best placed to address. Some will take the view that the possible world in which prejudice is largely absent is further away than the possible world in which serious crime is largely absent and that the serious crime-free world is thereby a step on the way to the systemic prejudice-free world. If that is the case, then it may also be the case that our political efforts are better focused on achieving the kind of deep change in attitudes that would be necessary for us to live as social equals. The damaging effects of undercover policing in any world with entrenched systematic prejudice undermine it as legitimate institution, and such worlds exist along the horizon.

The weakest part of this argument is the claim that the possibility in which serious crime is eliminated is a step on the way to the possibility in which systematic prejudice is eliminated. The argument holds that it is not worth hypothesising a world that lacks systemic prejudice but has policing, because a world without systemic prejudice would not need policing of serious crime. It may or may not be the case that this counterfactual is true, in the sense that the closest world without systemic prejudice lacks serious crime. It is difficult to assess it. But even if it is true, it does not undermine the exercise being put forward here. The goal is to set up an ideal, to understand what principles are at work, and it is useful in doing so to abstract away from institutional failures. Insofar as existing institutions do not meet both the standards of avoiding systematic prejudice, and also do not meet the standards that I argue for in this book, then they fail twice.

There is another sense in which the argument that I put forward here is a kind of ideal theory. A great deal of policing of organised crime involves working on impeding the markets in drugs. An account of the justifiability of harmful police tactics like undercover operations will need to make reference to the beneficial consequences of the practice. There are very serious questions about the evidence for the value of enforcing a prohibition on drugs. The so-called 'war on drugs' has its historical roots in a fearful and racialised culture that had recently failed to enforce a prohibition on alcohol, and arguably fear and prejudice have never been far from the surface in rationalisations of aggressive efforts at drug prohibition.[31] There is evidence that policing of substances for personal use tends to bring about, in the manner of evolution, a more violent culture within distribution networks; that it increases addiction through the criminalisation of users who would benefit from health treatment and compassion in addressing their addictions; and that it increases deaths from overdose through the incentivisation of the creation of purer chemicals and unregulated markets.[32] If the existing move towards legalisation continues,[33] then the policing of organised crime may look quite different in fifty years' time, since the central source of funding of crime will have been dramatically reduced. Moreover, while I will use examples involving drugs in this book, I do this with the motivation of drawing upon real life examples of the structure that an undercover operation may take. If one takes the view that drug laws are largely wrong-headed and unjust, then there will be an air of unreality about any discussion of ideal undercover policing.

However, I maintain that the structure of the norms that I put forward here is valid and has implications for how we should think about the here and now. The objection to undercover police *tout court* is best interpreted as a pragmatic one focusing on institutional integrity or on the challenges of reaching the ideal. The spirit of this book, in contrast, is in the realm of ideal theory. I proceed with the conviction that in order to understand better or worse policing, it is crucial to have an understanding of correct policing or legitimate policing. The challenge is to explain more closely when and why undercover work can be justifiable. Many will be keen to urge that this is a distant counterfactual, especially in the realm of undercover policing. However, I hope that the progress of the argument I put forward in this book will illustrate how it is useful to theorise ideally in seeking to understand our values: people want to understand what is more or less legitimate, or more or less fair.[34]

6   Against undercover police

The other objection to undercover work takes on the proper functioning of policing and seeks to drive a wedge between the two. That is, it claims that undercover tactics are incompatible with the proper function of police. There are competing accounts of the proper function of police, ranging from a focus on their role as coercive,[35] to their function as enforcers of people's moral and legal rights,[36] to a 'secret social service' function,[37] to a community-based role,[38] to straightforwardly retributivist or consequentialist or contractualist positions.[39] Versions of all of those views share one element: that legitimate policing is in some way *public*. For instance, it may be argued that people cannot legitimately be coerced without being party to the reasons behind the coercion. Legitimate policing is an expression of citizens' own will, and as such cannot be carried out in a way that is disconnected from their awareness. In order for an action to be an expression of citizens' will it is necessary – runs the argument – for citizens to be able to *know* what is purportedly done on their behalf. Undercover policing, in contrast, involves hiding from people that they are dealing with the police at all and the deliberate creation of other false beliefs in the people that they are dealing with.

It is unclear exactly what the requirement of publicity upon policing is. Let us attempt to construct the strongest possible version of the objection. The objection can be taken in one or both of two different ways, focusing either on effects, on beliefs, or on actions. It may be that the *deceptive* element of undercover policing is seen to be incompatible with the necessarily public nature of justified police activity, or it may be that the *manipulative* element of undercover policing is seen to be incompatible with the necessarily public nature of justified policing.

6.1 Deceiving citizens

Versions of the former argument hold that state agents should *never* deceive citizens or that they should *never* lie to citizens. How could we ever accept deliberate lying and dissembling by police? A simple, stark version of this argument holds that lying is wrong, especially when it is carried out by public officials towards citizens; undercover policing inherently involves lying by public officials towards citizens; therefore, undercover policing is not an acceptable tactic.

According to this argument, these are not merely *prima facie* or *pro tanto* wrongs. A *prima facie* wrong is a wrong that may be *defeated* by some other consideration. One might say that it is *prima facie* wrong to hurt others, but it is not wrong to do so in certain cases of self-defence. A *pro tanto* wrong is a wrong that may be *outweighed* by other considerations. Perhaps one should keep one's promises, but also, when keeping a small promise becomes vastly risky or costly, the obligation to do so may be dominated by other considerations. On the argument be considered here, deceptions or lies by state agents are almost always wrong all-things-considered: they are *prima facie* or *pro tanto* wrongs that are not defeated or outweighed.

Undercover officers are employed to deceive citizens about who they are.[40] They form connections with people that are deliberately built on falsehoods. Elaborate and plausible back-stories are created, and officers go to great lengths to ensure that those who come into contact with them while they are in role believe in these 'legends' and do not suspect their role as a state agent.

The wrong of lying is sometimes explicated with reference to the value of the practice of truth-telling. A social world in which this norm is abandoned is almost inconceivable. Insofar as such a world is conceivable, it is a highly impractical one. Harnessing this insight, Bok argues, in a manner reminiscent of Kant, that you ought not to lie just on the grounds that it would be convenient, since you ought, on reflection, to realise that you are not relevantly different from anybody else and that you do not wish that the norm against lying should be generally violated.[41] Undercover officers may provide one of the exceptions to this principle: as state agents who are charged with this kind of behaviour, they are in a 'relevant' way different from others. Shiffrin instead emphasises the damage that lying does to the system of truthfulness, and also the importance of that system not just in communication but also in our ability to think. Even when facing Kant's murderer at the door, who demands to know whether his desired victim is at home, Shiffrin argues that we should not lie in ways that 'strategically subvert the machinery of authentic communication' because 'such misrepresentations damage that machinery, and excommunicate their recipients from the moral community'.[42] On this argument, the objection to lying is *strengthened* when it is carried out by undercover officers, who, as state agents, are an element of the authority that has power over the ability of people to form patterns of communication. If our system of truth is fragile, we should be concerned, according to this argument, if *even police officers* are to act in ways that undermine it.

Deception is sometimes said to be a core part of policing in general. Many aspects of policing, such as interviewing, and strategising about resource deployment involve concealment, dissembling, deception, and lying.[43] This does not settle the matter by itself. The reply remains open that policing should thereby be largely abandoned or reconceived. While expressing something of the impermissibility of deceitful state agents, the argument that police lies or deceptions are always all-things-considered wrongs rests on an implausibly strong principle. Just as we tend to seek exceptions to the rule against lying when the would-be murderer knocks at the door asking for the whereabouts of his target, we will also allow exceptions to the rules against lying and deception by the state in emergencies. A more plausible principle is that state agents should never deceive or lie to citizens, except in emergencies, and where other methods that do not involve lying or deception (or involve comparable harms) are unavailable. This becomes an argument against undercover policing if the relevant emergencies are very rare, or if, where they do arise, alternative non-deceitful methods are available.

Do (ideally understood) police deal with the relevant kinds of emergencies? The answer appears to be yes. A core part of the police role is precisely to address threats of serious harm, and in the context of the present discussion, the threats from serious organised crime might be taken often to provide the analogue to the murderer at the door. The argument will then turn to the question of whether other methods are preferable.

What are the likely other possible methods that may replace undercover operations? Some argue that, especially for 'secretive consensual crime', policing is impossible without the use of undercover work.[44] Nonetheless, often, one possible alternative approach is surveillance.[45] Surveillance will often, but not always, involve some degree of deception or dissembling (about who is listening to or watching the target) and will typically not involve lying. As an intelligence or evidence-gathering strategy, it is more efficacious where the target is helped to believe that they are not under surveillance, although no outright statement of falsehood will usually be necessary. (If the goal is to inhibit and disrupt, as may be the case in the policing of an online black market, then surveillance is more effective where the targets are led to believe that it is being used – although the effect will be heightened if there is ambiguity about exactly when and how extensively it is taking place.) It might then be argued that although police deception and dissembling is permissible, police lying is always wrong, and that surveillance is thereby, in ethical terms, usually a far superior tactic to undercover operations.

In reality, surveillance will sometimes be deployed as part of an undercover operation, sometimes with the undercover officer as a conduit for a recording device with the goal of obtaining evidence. Moreover, it will typically be attempted before undercover work, in part as a way of showing that an undercover operation is necessary, and in part because it is usually cheaper and less risky. It is only in the cases in which mere surveillance alone cannot reach the target that undercover work becomes an efficient use of police resources. Perhaps a vastly expanded system of surveillance could overcome these obstacles: technologically driven intrusions into all conversations, analysed in the first instance by sophisticated artificial intelligence, might provide a way to avoid having state agents lie to citizens, while still disrupting organised crime. This raises the possibility that it may be preferable for state agents to lie to some members of the population who are believed to be involved in wrongdoing, than it is for all citizens to undergo highly intrusive surveillance. Moreover, this possibility puts into question, again, the lexical priority of the value of having state agents never lie to citizens, in this case, putting it in competition with the value of privacy.[46] Why would it be the case that state lying is almost never acceptable, while at the same time it is very often permissible for the state to engage in acts of deception and dissembling relating to facts that people would find relevant (such as whether they are now being listened to)?

Aside from surveillance, informant use is another possible alternative strategy to undercover policing. In some forms, it looks similar to undercover work, where the informant is paid for intelligence over a long period and is encouraged to become more embedded in the organisation that is being infiltrated. In other forms, it is somewhat different: the informant is motivated by the possibility of avoiding or diminishing criminal charges, or a sense of responsibility or revenge, or by the value of a relationship with their handler.[47] Any or all of these motivations may be at work in each case. In whatever way they are motivated, informants lie to citizens just as undercover agents do.[48] Perhaps it is worse for state agents to lie to citizens themselves than it is for state agents to pay or otherwise encourage citizens to lie to one another. Even so, it seems hard to make the case that the former is ruled out absolutely or nearly absolutely, while the latter is permissible and can be widely instituted. How can we make the case that *lying* is especially bad, over and above the causing of false beliefs? In the case of the informant, we have someone in the same role but who is not a police officer. Why is *causing* a person to be lied to ok, but not *lying* to a person?

There are some possible moral advantages of undercover over informant use. The risk is taken on by the state agent rather than pressed upon the vulnerable, and so too are the moral and psychological costs of the action. This may be preferable because the state agent can be given a structure that will make them more resilient and because they freely sign up for this kind of profession.

In general, lying may be regarded as generally immoral, especially where it is carried out by state agents, but so, too, is the use of force and coercion. If force and coercion by state agents can be justified in some circumstances, perhaps in response to some types of action, then it is difficult to see why lying cannot be so justified.

6.2 *Manipulating citizens*

A different version of the incoherence objection to undercover policing focuses on the manipulative element, holding that manipulation is inconsistent with proper police function. A powerful argument against stings in general is put forward by Jeffrey Howard. On his view, the 'moral subversion account' encouraging others to become wrongdoers is *prima facie* wrong. The grounding for this idea is the Rawlsian notion that we have a first-order duty to respect people's moral powers, one of which is the ability to act rightly. Howard's position is that one wrongs a person by inducing her to commit a wrong, even if it is a wrong that she will be responsible for. As Howard puts it: 'By acting in ways that increase the likelihood that Carl's moral capacities will malfunction, Barry is failing to relate to Carl in the way that moral agents ought to relate to one another.'[49] We might take Howard's idea and put it in the context of our present argument by saying that it is incompatible with police function for them to relate to citizens in this way.

It is worth noting the broadness of the application of Howard's argument. It does not just apply to manipulations, where a certain kind of act is procured through non-rational means. Including and extending beyond this, moral subversion refers to actions that 'increase the likelihood' that another will commit a wrong.[50] Thus, some undercover policing, such as the non-pushy sting, is not manipulative at all, or only minimally manipulative. Nonetheless, presenting a person with the criminal opportunity involved in a non-pushy sting *does* increase the chance that a person will commit a wrong, and so is morally subversive, in Howard's terms.

While it powerfully expresses one of the *prima facie* wrongs of undercover policing, this argument faces similar problems to the argument from lying that we considered in the previous section. The reason that moral subversion is wrongful is that it involves relating to people in the wrong kind of way. Once again, it is extreme to claim that it is unacceptable in any circumstances to relate to people in the wrong way. Rather, we might say that state agents should never lead people into wrongdoing, *except in emergencies*, and where other methods that do not lead people into wrongdoing (or involve comparable harms) are unavailable. Since organised crime often does present us with the core of an emergency, the issue turns, as it did in the discussion in the previous section, to whether the harms of undercover policing are less palatable than the harms caused by other forms of policing. As Richard Lippke puts it, there may be 'principles of comparable or greater weight' than the principle of avoiding moral subversion.[51]

Lying, deception, and manipulation by state agents are serious *prima facie* wrongs, and will require very good justifications, given their inherent tension with the imperative of state agents to be *public*, in the sense that I have discussed in this section. Given the sophistication of and damage done by serious organised crime, however, it is a bold step to argue that such justifications never or only in very rare can cases be made – although the possibility remains open, and the answer will ultimately depend in part on a moral assessment of alternative strategies as well as the damage done by these organisations and possibilities of disrupting them.

Notes

1 Home Affairs Committee. Minutes of Evidence HC 837. https://publications. parliament.uk/pa/cm201213/cmselect/cmhaff/837/130205i.htm.

2 Goldstein, Joseph. 'Police Discretion Not to Invoke the Criminal Process: Low-Visibility Decisions in the Administration of Justice'. Yale Law Journal (1960): 543–94; Ohlin, Lloyd E., and Frank J. Remington, eds. Discretion in Criminal Justice: The Tension between Individualization and Uniformity. Albany: State University of New York Press, 1993; Kleinig, John, ed. Handled with Discretion: Ethical Issues in Police Decision Making. London: Rowman & Littlefield, 1996.

3 Loftus, B. 'Normalizing Covert Surveillance: The Subterranean World of Policing'. British Journal of Sociology 6 March 2019. In the UK, it is reported that the use of 'CHIS' (Covert Human Intelligence Sources) is decreasing somewhat. (Investigatory Powers Commissioner's Annual Report 2019, p. 78.) However, the category includes informants and undercover police together, and the longer term trend in undercover policing appears to be upwards.

4 Willis, James J. 'A Recent History of the Police'. In The Oxford Handbook of Police and Policing. Oxford: Oxford University Press, 2014, pp. 3–33, p. 22.

5 Marx, Gary T. Undercover: Police Surveillance in America. Berkeley: University of California Press, 1988.

6 The view I put forward builds upon the position I advance in Nathan, C. 'Liability to Deception and Manipulation: The Ethics of Undercover Policing'. Journal of Applied Philosophy 34, no. 3 (2017): 370–88.

7 For a more detailed definition of 'covert human intelligence sources' (which includes informants), see the UK Regulation of Investigatory Powers Act (2000), s.26.

8 I discuss manipulation further in chapter 5.

9 Further, there may be legitimate police functions that do not make reference to criminal activity, but which may be addressed undercover. For example, if managing and improving community relations is a part of the proper police role, such work could be carried out undercover.

10 The UK regime, thus, brings undercover officers and informants within the same category.

11 Gregory, Julia. 'How Council Uses Spies to Watch Benefit Cheats and Rogue Traders in One London Borough'. MyLondon, 2018. www. mylondon.news/news/west-london-news/how-council-uses-spies-watch- 15503070.

12 Smith, Dave, and Phil Chamberlain. Blacklisted. Oxford: New Internationalist, 2017; Lubbers, Eveline. Secret Manoeuvres in the Dark. London: Pluto Press, 2012.

13 See the 'Stardust Jewellers' case, R v Bryce, Court Of Appeal, Criminal Division [1992] 4 All ER 567, 95 Cr App Rep 320; 'Defendants in Jewellery Shop "Sting" Sentenced'. Independent, 23 January 1993. www.i ndependent.co.uk/news/uk/defendants-in-jewellery-shop-sting-sentenced- 1480161.html (accessed November 2021).

14 For a classic conceptual scheme of undercover policing, identifying the three possible purposes of intelligence, prevention, and facilitation, see Marx, Gary T. Undercover: Police Surveillance in America. Berkeley: University of California Press, 1988. Here I draw upon this rich schema.

15 When an officer facilitates a path for a criminal act, it remains an open question whether entrapment is occurring, since that path may be been present event absent the officer's actions.

16 Webster, D. W., M. T. Bulzacchelli, A. M. Zeoli, and J. S. Vernick. 'Effects of Undercover Police Stings of Gun Dealers on the Supply of New Guns to Criminals'. Injury Prevention 12, no. 4 (1 August 2006): 225–30.

17 For a discussion of the tension between the goals of deterrence and obtaining information in stings, see Hay, Bruce. 'Sting Operations, Undercover Agents, and Entrapment'. Modern Law Review. 70 (2005): 387.

18 See Wachtel, Julius. 'From Morals to Practice: Dilemmas of Control in Undercover Policing'. Crime, Law and Social Change 18, nos. 1–2 (1992): 137–58.

19 Dees, Tim. 'Here's the Hardest Part about Being an Undercover Cop'. Business Insider, 30 April 2014.

20 Marx, Gary T. 'Who Really Gets Stung? Some Issues Raised by the New Police Undercover Work'. Crime & Delinquency 28, no. 2 (1982): 166–7. See also Marx, Gary T. Undercover: Police Surveillance in America. Berkeley: University of California Press, 1988, p. 9.

21 Marx, Undercover, p. 61.

22 'Mark Townsend Investigates the Case of Paedophile Timothy Cox'. The Guardian, 9 September 2007. www.theguardian.com/society/2007/sep/09/childrensservices.

23 Home Office. Child Exploitation and Online Protection Centre (CEOP): The Way Forward. London: Stationery Office, 2010, p. 10. https://assets.publishing.service.gov.uk/government/uploads/system/uploads/attachment_data/file/228968/7785.pdf.

24 Ohr, Bruce G. 'Effective Methods to Combat Transnational Organized Crime in Criminal Justice Processes'. 116th International Training Course, Visiting Experts Papers, October, 1999, p. 48.

25 Kleinig, John. The Ethics of Policing. Cambridge: Cambridge University Press, 1996. See also Kleinig, J. Ends and Means in Policing. Abingdon, UK: Routledge, 2019. Of course, in policy terms, a good regime will require that police rely on specific criteria like the prevention of a crime.

26 Vitale, Alex S. The End of Policing. London and New York: Verso Books, 2017, p. 30.

27 See also Wertheimer, Roger. 'Are the Police Necessary?'. In The Police in Society. D.C. Heath, 1975.

28 Vitale, The End of Policing, p. 133.

29 Peeples, L. 'What the Data Say about Police Brutality and Racial Bias: And Which Reforms Might Work'. Nature 583 (July 2020); Evans, R. 'Met Faces Legal Action over Spies' Use of Dead Children's Identities'.

Guardian, 7 December 2020. www.theguardian.com/uk-news/2020/dec/07/met-police-legal-action-spies-use-dead-childrens-identities.

30 Cohen, G. A. Rescuing Justice and Equality. Cambridge, MA: Harvard University Press, 2008.

31 Stuntz, William J. 'Race, Class, and Drugs'. Columbia Law Review 98, no. 1795 (1998); Tonry, Michael. 'Race and the War on Drugs'. University of Chicago Legal Forum 1994 (1994): 25.

32 Taylor, S., J. Buchanan, and T. Ayres. 'Prohibition, Privilege and the Drug Apartheid: The Failure of Drug Policy Reform to Address the Underlying Fallacies of Drug Prohibition'. Criminology & Criminal Justice 16, no. 4 (2016): 452–69. Husak, Douglas, and Peter de Marneffe. The Legalization of Drugs: For and Against. Cambridge and New York: Cambridge University Press, 2006. A powerful popular account of these arguments is Hari, Johann. Chasing the Scream: The First and Last Days of the War on Drugs. Bloomsbury, 2015.

33 Bacon, Matthew. 'Desistance from Criminalisation: Police Culture and New Directions in Drugs Policing'. Policing and Society, May 2021.

34 Whereas police abolitionists tend to focus on recent and ongoing scandals and systemic problems in policing, there is a more principled kind of opposition to policing that I will not address directly in this short book. One may take a libertarian or anarchist line that little or no policing is justified, on the grounds that police powers infringe people's rights, and is not and cannot be consented to. Again, the aspiration is that the position put forward in chapters 3 and 4 provides a powerful model that appropriately takes on board the relevant norms.

35 Bittner, Egon. Functions of the Police in Modern Society. New York: Jason Aronson, 1978.

36 Miller, Seumas. The Moral Foundations of Social Institutions: A Philosophical Study. Cambridge: Cambridge University Press, 2010.

37 Millie, Andrew. 'What Are the Police for?' In The Future of Policing, edited by J. M. Brown, 2013, pp. 52–63.

38 Cordner, Gary. 'Community Policing'. In The Oxford Handbook of Police and Policing, edited by Michael D. Reisig and Robert J. Kane. Oxford: Oxford University Press, 2014.

39 Kleinig, John. The Ethics of Policing. Cambridge: Cambridge University Press, 1996.

40 To be sure, the citizens are typically believed to be involved in wrongdoing – a point that I return to in chapter 2 and continue to discuss for the remainder of this text.

41 Bok, Sissela. Lying: Moral Choice in Public and Private Life. Updated edition. New York: Vintage Books USA, 1999.

42 Shiffrin, Seana Valentine. Speech Matters: On Lying, Morality, and the Law. Carl G. Hempel Lecture Series. Princeton: Princeton University Press, 2014.

43 Kleinig emphasises the range of kinds of deception, and how it goes beyond straightforward lying. Kleinig, John. The Ethics of Policing.

Cambridge: Cambridge University Press, 1996. See also Alpert, Geoffrey P., and Jeffrey J. Noble. 'Lies, True Lies, and Conscious Deception: Police Officers and the Truth'. Police Quarterly 12, no. 2 (1 June 2009): 237–54.

44 Marx, Gary T. Undercover: Police Surveillance in America. Berkeley: University of California Press, 1988. See also Wachtel, 'From Morals to Practice', 137–58.

45 Sheptycki, James. 'Editorial Reflections on Surveillance and Intelligence-Led Policing'. Policing and Society 9, no. 4 (1 January 2000): 311–14, and the accompanying issue.

46 There is an abstraction in this argument. We are considering the ethics of undercover policing and surveillance. There is also a politics of undercover policing and surveillance. Some will focus on the trustworthiness of state institutions, arguing that the power that is associated with some forms of surveillance or policing power will tend to concentrate, self-justify, and grow. These aren't arguments that I consider here.

47 Billingsley, Roger, Teresa Nemitz, and Philip Bean, eds. Informers: Policing, Policy, Practice. Abingdon, UK: Routledge, 2013; Hewitt, Steve. Snitch!: A History of the Modern Intelligence Informer. New York and London: Continuum, 2010; Natapoff, Alexandra. Snitching: Criminal Informants and the Erosion of American Justice. New York and London: New York University Press, 2009.

48 Those correctly believed to be involved in serious wrongs are, of course, still citizens. I discuss the idea that people make themselves liable to such treatment in the bulk of this book.

49 Howard, Jeffrey W. 'Moral Subversion and Structural Entrapment'. Journal of Political Philosophy (1 August 2015): 6.

50 Howard places a caveat upon this principle, whereby 'morally protected' actions, such as those protected by freedom of speech or association, are not morally subversive.

51 Lippke, Richard L. 'A Limited Defense of What Some Will Regard as Entrapment'. Legal Theory 23, no. 4 (2017): 283–306, p. 292.

2   The challenge of justification

1   Policing wrongs

In this chapter, I take a closer look at the *prima facie* wrongs involved
in undercover policing. I then consider three possibilities in justifying them. The first position takes a pluralist approach, shying away
from combining the different factors at stake, instead letting them
stand on their own terms. The second position, the 'instrumentalist'
view, takes the opposite tack, holding that we should weight up the
costs and benefits and that undercover policing is justified when and
only when the latter outweigh the former. Third, the 'consent' view
holds that the *prima facie* wrongs of undercover policing are justified because we consent to them.

We have seen in Chapter 1 how undercover policing involves the
prima facie wrongs of *deception* and *manipulation*. Even if these
may be justified all-things-considered, they demand justification.
They are *prima facie* wrongs. That is, they are wrong on the face
of things, but the wrongness may be cancelled by some other circumstance.[1] Furthermore, they are *pro tanto* wrongs. That is, the
wrongness may be outweighed by some concurrent good, making
the action justified on balance.[2]

Alongside deception and manipulation, we should also add two
further *prima facie* wrongs. First, undercover policing can impose
direct harms upon people. These can be psychological harms,
changes in the direction of a person's life, or even assaults on a person's physical integrity. At the extreme, officers can form intimate
bonds with and have children with the people that they are tasked to

DOI: 10.4324/9780429293443-2

spy upon. One subject of such spying described her experience in the following terms:

> I feel cheated. I feel I was violated, in a cruel way. It's almost like rape really, when I look back, that's how I feel the extent of the way I was used. Almost like a prostitute – he had his 'real' relationship; he was married with children.[3]

There are less serious direct harms of undercover work. Where a police officer acting undercover forms an ongoing personal friendship with a person, one of the harms that is imposed is the straightforward rerouting of that person's life. Those who are the subject of long-term infiltrations might rightly complain that time put into building bonds with a person has been wasted, and there is an accompanying opportunity cost. Some targets of undercover work will draw a great deal from the apparently genuine interest that the officer provides, and will accordingly invest in the friendship in return. On exit, the friendship ends, and the social investment is lost. Of course, personal relationships wax and wane in the normal run of things, and many are fleeting by design. By setting a hidden time limit on the friendship, however, an officer can extract a great deal of an individual's social energy and time, and this is energy that could be invested elsewhere.

Corruption of personal relationships can have serious direct psychological effects on a person. Where the falsehood of the relationship is eventually revealed, it can carry form of trauma. Those who have been subject to undercover operations sometimes talk of the impossibility of believing, on some level, that the officer really was simply acting. An important development of this undermining of harm to personal relationships is that once the harm is known about, it will also damage future relationships, since having been the target of such an operation will affect people's future ability to trust others.

Alongside these direct harms (to psychology, to course of life, and to bodily integrity), undercover policing also carries the *prima facie* wrong of intrusion of privacy. Accounts of privacy differ on how to conceive of intrusions as *prima facie* wrongful. Undercover policing is not qualitatively distinguished from surveillance in this regard, although the forms of intrusion will tend to be more intense. Claims to privacy are plausibly understood as bundles of different claims. Among these are rights to control over property and interests in developing personal spaces.[4] For the purposes of this book, I will remain neutral on the content of the claims that privacy involves, aiming instead to establish the case that *whatever* one's understanding of the setbacks that intrusions impose, from a wide range of plausible possibilities, our governance of such intrusions should be expressly sensitive to culpability. Indeed, some will hold that privacy is an essentially social value. On this view, widespread intrusions weaken a set of conventions that benefit us all, and these conventions are only explicable in the context of their joint expression.[5] The framework I put forward here is consistent with this view, so long as we can conceive of a vast range of intrusions as actions that impose setbacks not just upon social values but also individual interests.[6]

2 Collateral harms

Aside from the *prima facie* wrongs described previously, there are a number of setbacks imposed by undercover tactics that fall upon people other than those who are immediately targeted by undercover operations or who interact with undercover officers. The interests that are affected can be straightforwardly financial. Fake fences can have effects on people's businesses, and indeed upon businesses that are not part of the operation.[7] Stings can create crimes, as where police set up a business aimed at buying stolen goods, an effect may be to encourage burglary:

> two young men learned that a local 'fence' – in reality a police sting – was buying stolen cars. They stole several cars and sold them to the sting. They showed the undercover officers a .45 caliber automatic taken in a burglary, stole another car, killed its owner in the process with this gun, and then sold the car to the 'fence'. They repeated this again and were then arrested.[8]

Furthermore, those who are not targeted by undercover officers but who rationally suspect that they may be targeted will undergo a version of the setback associated with the breaking of trust.[9] Consider a political protest group whose members seek to build a movement that acts within the criminal law. It organises rallies in cooperation with the police, it builds networks with relevant individuals and groups, and it lobbies. Suppose there has been high profile infiltration by the police of other networks of protesters. The knowledge of this infiltration has a chilling effect upon this lawful movement. Its existing members are slower to trust one another than they otherwise would be, and they are slower to incorporate new members within their leading ranks. One of the many exceptions to the slogan 'if you have nothing to hide, then you have nothing to fear' is applicable in such a case.[10] Undercover officers can temporarily make good members of a protest group – they will tend to be relatively well-resourced and enthusiastic – but they are liable to disappear suddenly, and they will have some reason to encourage its more radical and lawfully questionable elements, independently of the group's own good strategy. The use of undercover police in one area, then, can be expected to have effects on others who are acting lawfully.

A more egregious kind of collateral harm involves the adoption by undercover officers of birth certificates of deceased citizens, especially those who died in childhood. Such documents provide cover, as they allow officers to show a genuine birth certificate to any who should suspect them.[11] When such actions are made public, they can be expected to have a traumatising effect upon the families of those whose identities have been used. If the use of such birth certificates is kept secret, it remains the case that the practice institutionalises a police role in undermining respect for the deceased and in deceiving third parties about doing so.

The institution of undercover police also can cause harms to those who serve as officers. They expose themselves to a risk of physical harm.[12] Officers are especially likely to come to harm where they are infiltrating organisations that are comfortable with violence. Furthermore, by training them to live double lives, their psychology can be deeply altered by their profession. It is normal for ex-officers to talk about the psychological strains that they undergo. One officer described to this author having undergone a mock execution at the hands of an IRA cell as a way of testing whether he would 'show out'. A long-term undercover officer describes how it 'was normal practice after finishing an operation to harbour different feelings: thoughts of betrayal, divided loyalties and a sense of sadness'.[13] Another writes:

> An ideal UC is an amiable type who makes friends easily. You can fake that just so much. Spend enough time with people

who like and trust you, doing what they do, and you're likely to develop some affection for them, even though what they do goes against your moral principles. When the time comes that you have to betray their trust and take part in their undoing, there is a real sense of betrayal. UCs who are 'under' for prolonged periods – years, sometimes – often need psychological counseling to deal with the conflict.[14]

To be sure, it should be noted, ex-officers commonly also report gaining a great deal from their work.[15]

3   The *prima facie* wrongs of two kinds of undercover policing

I have described five headings of *prima facie* wrongs of undercover policing:

1   Direct harms: integrity, time, and trauma
2   Manipulation
3   Deception
4   Intrusion
5   Harms upon third parties, police officers

This is not to say that these effects cannot be mitigated or by themselves render undercover operations unjustified. The point is that these are a feature of the ethical landscape. It is of special interest in this book how these *prima facie* wrongs might be justifiable. Consider now how these wrongs can apply to the two different paradigmatic forms of undercover policing described in Chapter 1. Recall, these are the *sting* and *infiltration*. I distinguished these forms of undercover policing according to how active or passive they are: whether they have an effect on the world, whether they work to infiltrate, or to immediately prevent or catch crime. Stings and infiltration will both tend to carry the third-party harms referred to under heading 5. The effects upon public social structures and the criminal justice system result from the distrust created by police deceptions. Insofar as infiltrations tend to involve undercover officers going deeper into their roles, they will be more likely to threaten harm to them – but stings are also not risk-free. Immediate third parties may tend to be affected by the sting element of an operation, as markets in some good will tend to be distorted. But infiltrations can also have serious effects upon the innocent associates of targets (a topic that we discuss in Chapter 4).

An active sting will involve all of the *prima facie* wrongs numbered 1–4 earlier: direct harms, manipulation, deception, and intrusion. It takes up the time of the targets, it guides their behaviour, the targets are deceived about who they are dealing with, and their personal life is intruded upon by the officer. A passive sting, on the other hand, may be only minimally manipulative, as it does not present a novel opportunity, and it may be only minimally intrusive, as little is learned about the targets beyond their purchasing choice. These are general tendencies, of course, and the specific assessment will depend on each case. Here, one can note that there are possible stings that primarily engage the *prima facie* wrongs of deception and direct harms, and much less so manipulation and intrusion.

Active infiltrations will similarly tend to engage all of the *prima facie* wrongs set out earlier. In guiding behaviour, they are inherently manipulative; as with all undercover work, they deceive about the nature of the officer; they occupy the time and mind of the target; and they depend upon and often aim at learning more about the target's private life. Passive infiltrations, on the other hand, may be only minimally manipulative in obtaining a permit to work in a certain part of an office, and may take up little of people's life as they function in the manner of a listening device. Like a listening device, the central issue is the intrusion involved.

4   Dirty hands

Faced with the costs and benefits described in this and the previous chapter, the key question of principle is, how should we reconcile them? One popular answer to that question that is popularly appealed to across the political debate on the topic, whether by those who are apologists or opponents of the tactic, says that there is an irrevocable wrong committed by the police when they act undercover, but it is a wrong that is incommensurate with the significant goods of crime prevention and the prosecution of those who commit wrongs.[16] That is to say, undercover work is a case of dirty hands. As one undercover police officer said when asked about the ethics of his work, 'that's like trying to invent dry water or fireproof coal'.[17] The view often attributed to Machiavelli is that power inevitably involves doing some things that are wrongs, arising from genuine moral dilemmas. We must accept this moral residue, but we also do better not to dwell on our misdeeds. On this view, committing moral wrongs is part of the core of undercover work. The best we can do is to embrace the values we gain: in this case, the reduction of crime and the increase in security. It retains, nonetheless, a tragic element, since it is necessary that the work is performed, and those who perform it commit wrongs, thereby performing a sacrifice.[18]

The background meta-ethics of such a view would involve a form of value pluralism, whereby there are multiple values – such as the security of the population from crime and the freedom from particular individuals from the harms listed earlier, such as the freedom from state interference in one's personal life – and that these various values can, and frequently do, come into conflict with one another. Further, on this view, there is no general way of resolving these conflicts. The values are frequently incommensurable or incomparable.[19] They cannot be measured on the same scale, and there is no greatest good against which the rest are measured.

Thus, Isaiah Berlin argues that, of necessity, we cannot have everything when it comes to politics. In places, justice may conflict with beauty, or liberty with truth, or happiness with equality, or indeed security with liberty. Things are what they are, and attempts to subsume some values under others are therefore bound to fail.

There is a strong pragmatic objection to the dirty hands account of undercover policing. That is to say, there is an objection that is grounded not directly in its substantive accuracy as a theory but in the usefulness of taking it on board. Pragmatic objections of this type are not decisive. It may be the case that the truth is a damaging, dangerous, or difficult thing to know. But such objections have *pro tanto* force. They direct the way that theoretical scrutiny may best run, and how intensely to seek alternatives.

The pragmatic objection has two parts. First, one can reasonably expect that the effects of an internalisation of a dirty hands ethic by agents of a practice that is inherently secretive would be to encourage further secretiveness. A belief on the part of its agents that the practice is not wrongful is more conducive to public justification and regulation. We discussed earlier the possibility that by engaging in deception at one part of the criminal justice process, police officers may take on a 'subcultural norm' in which norms against deception in other parts of the criminal justice process become destabilised. If this is true for consequentialist reasoning about deception, it is likely to be true for wrongs in general.

Second, a public that takes on board this view of manipulative policing will correctly feel that it puts wrongful acts at the centre of police practice. The wrongs may be justified by appeal to necessity, but unease will remain.

Even if pluralism is the correct description of the moral universe, then, we should, for pragmatic reasons, avoid the dirty hands description of undercover policing if we can.

5   Instrumental justifications

An alternative view holds that covert work is justified where (and only where) its harms are outweighed by its benefits. Call this the 'instrumental' model.[20] The instrumental model is in evidence in its purest form in contexts that are adjacent to undercover policing. Consider foreign signals intelligence. As General Michael Hayden, former head of the US National Security Agency, said, 'I am simply going out there to retrieve information that helps keep my countrymen free and safe. This is not about guilt. . . . NSA doesn't just listen to bad people. NSA listens to *interesting* people.'[21] In foreign intelligence, there is no strong or established practice of due process. Rather, the focus is upon efficacy. The answer to the question of whether or not resources, including privacy-intruding resources, should be expended in one area rather than another is determined by the outcome of a cost-benefit analysis.

What if this set of norms were extended from foreign signals intelligence into the domestic context involving undercover agents? Such a state of affairs has precedent. Consider the historic involvement of the intelligence services in the British Communist Party:

> In the international communist movement, the British party was a laughing stock, correctly assumed to be so thoroughly penetrated that it was virtually a branch of the Security Service. As Roger Hollis [Director General of MI5] told the home secretary in 1959, 'we [have] the British Communist Party pretty well

buttoned up'. It was more than mere containment, says [David] Cornwell [MI5/MI6 Officer], who ran agents into the party. 'We kept it afloat. In fact, we owned it.'[22]

Around half a million files were made on communists or communist sympathisers, of which twenty thousand were members of the British Communist Party – but of all these, only a few were ever prosecuted. How are we to interpret these numbers? A justification of this practice would have to begin within what I am calling the instrumental view. The use of security resources in order to spy on people in virtue of their political views, without any aspiration towards criminal prosecution, could only be explained on the grounds that the practice serves some more general security aims.

I do not claim that the instrumental view will inevitably involve intrusions upon citizens on such a wide scale. The widespread intrusion on political groups might be objected to within the instrumentalist structure. Indeed, some make the case that intrusive security work in general is poor value for money, and that a pure cost-benefit analysis will tend to show that the resources it absorbs would be better spent elsewhere.[23] My claim is that it is difficult to see the activity of the intelligence services in the aforementioned contexts in any way other than as an effort to implement an instrumentalist view.

Regardless of the aforementioned cases, the instrumental view is not attractive in principle. Whereas the dirty hands view clings too firmly to the status of covert policing as wrongful, the instrumental view is uncomfortably blasé. Intrusions by undercover police can take place against people who are not believed to be involved in any wrongdoing. A stark example is in the FBI's effort to locate fugitives from the Weather Underground faction of Students for a Democratic Society:

> A federal agent posing as a radical infiltrated a student milieu thought to be close to this faction. He developed a relationship with a political activist, and she became pregnant. After considerable indecision, and at the urging of the agent, she had an abortion. His efforts did not locate the fugitive. The agent's work then took him elsewhere, and he ended the relationship. The woman apparently never learned of his secret identity and true motives.[24]

That is an extreme case. But now know such a similar practice occurred in the UK over a number of years.[25]

On behalf of the instrumental view, it may be objected that the benefits of the actions of the officer could not be expected to outweigh their very serious costs. However, I add to this argument a further objection that is *inconsistent* with the instrumental view: that no special consideration appears to have been given to the non-culpability of the target.

Secondary intrusions of a less powerful kind are likely to be extremely common: 'A typical undercover operation with strong intelligence aimed at drug trafficking will enable officers to draw up a detailed picture of the private lives of those involved, and their associates, innocent or otherwise.'[26] The trouble with the instrumental view is that it gives no direct differential ethical consideration to those who are (a) useful targets who are acting criminally; (b) useful targets who are not criminal or otherwise wrongful actors; and (c) those affected collaterally by the targeting of others. Intuitively, those are different cases. Holding constant the advantage gained in terms of policing function, it is intuitive that the first of those categories are more liable to intrusions than the second and the third. But the instrumental view makes no such distinction. If, for example, a small amount of security gain can be achieved by imposing either a high cost upon people who are not believed to be involved in any wrongdoing, or the same cost upon those who are, then the instrumental view is indifferent. This seems mistaken.

6   Consent to undercover policing

Where policing is carried out justly and legitimately, it involves actions to which citizens have consented. The ideal of policing by consent is often put forward. The consent argument says: ideally, we all commit, collectively and democratically, to the institution of the police. This commitment is one that we can properly make together. And in so committing, we agree that police act only in certain ways. We also agree to accept some actions on the part of the police that will set back some people's interests, including the interests of those who have not committed any wrong and do not intend to do so. Having consented to the institution, then if it functions in the way that it is expected to, people lack a complaint when it imposes setbacks upon them. This includes where, for example, it sets up a fake business that somewhat undermines a legitimate one; it intrudes upon the privacy of an individual who turns out to be irrelevant but upon whom suspicion fell; and so forth.

Consider the following example. An officer, accompanying his target, enters into a cafe and, on ordering, has a conversation with a waiter, who knows the target as a regular, but is not under any suspicion. The conversation is friendly, and the officer ingratiates himself with the waiter, taking the opportunity to allude to and develop his credibility in the perception of the target. The officer and his target leave, and there is no more interaction with the waiter throughout the rest of the operation. The waiter, who is entirely innocent, has been deceived by a state agent in a relatively small way: the officer has lied to him and deliberately created further false beliefs. These are not important false beliefs, and he will soon forget them, as he forgets many of the beliefs that he has about his clientele. It remains the case that a state agent has lied to and more broadly deceived the waiter, has manipulated him, and may have intruded upon his privacy.

On one view, a version of the dirty hands view, the waiter has suffered a wrong, all-things-considered. It may be a small wrong, but it is not straightforwardly eliminated as other factors such as the good that comes from the operation. The trouble with this reading of the case is that it expands to a very broad range of small and trivial state intrusions and sees a great mass of tiny state wrongs. Consider those who are videoed as part of a directed surveillance operation, or those who are recorded on CCTV but who are not involved in any wrongdoing. It seems independently odd to assert that these intrusions are all wrongs, even if they are justified. Furthermore, the view is unsatisfying for the reasons that the dirty hands view is unsatisfying; it sees a great many acts by police as wrongs. Yet further, the view may have the strange implication that people can claim recompense for such practices, even where they are justified all-things-considered.[27]

A better view provides an account of why there is not a wrong in such cases. Consent appears to perform such a role. One can agree to suffer harms or setbacks, especially when these are small. We consent on public transport or in contact sports to a chance of treatment that would in other contexts be assault. We consent to or sacrifice a complaint against certain forms of manipulation when we enter a department store.[28] So also, we consent in daily life to a chance of being deceived in trivial or small ways as a part of undercover operations that meet other justificatory criteria, such as that they provide an overwhelming security benefit. It seems reasonable to say that a risk of the waiter's treatment is the kind of thing that one agrees to as part of a democratic policing regime. On the consent reasoning, the waiter consents to a risk of such deceptions.

The example of the waiter suggests that the consent idea is especially attractive when we consider low-level policing setbacks. However, it has less force when it is applied to more significant policing harms. I have suggested that we can consent to harmful policing that meets *other justificatory criteria*. What are the other justificatory criteria? Where the harms are low, consent provides a significant part of the explanation of the justification of the action. If the operation is broadly beneficial, we might say to those who suffer small setbacks that the chance of such treatment is justified by the way that we together institute police as part of a system of collective protection. To those who suffer larger setbacks, however, we need to explain more closely just what kind of institution we have created. We have seen that the instrumental view is inadequate because it does not distinguish between harms to the liable and the non-liable. The consent idea is compatible with such a distinction, and is also compatible with its denial. To what regime do we collectively consent? Presumably, it is a regime that does require a stronger justification for intrusions upon those who are not suspected of any wrongdoing. In the next chapters we examine what this means.

The problem, then, with seeing undercover policing as justified only by its social contractual legitimacy is that it is a coherent possibility that people might contract into things that are not enforceable on the grounds that the contents of the contract involve one party committing a wrongdoing. There must, as it were, be something *behind* the contract, some other value at work. The matter cannot be consent all the way down, since there remains the question of what we can or should consent to. As Hume says: 'We are bound to obey our sovereign, it is said; because we have given a tacit promise to that purpose. But why are we bound to observe our promise?'[29] At the same time, I suggest that consent can provide a significant part of the explanation for why people lack a complaint where they suffer only minor setbacks in the course of otherwise justified undercover policing operations, since we are more likely to accept personal preference as decisive in cases of small setbacks, and consent here functions against a background in which such agreements are grounded.

To be sure, if consent is to play even this relatively small role, it remains to be shown just what kind is at work. Do people in fact agree to undercover policing institutions – perhaps tacitly, in virtue of accepting the benefits of state security, or more explicitly, such as participation in or accepting the benefits of an (ideal) democratic procedure? Or is it enough to show only that people consent in some relevant hypothetical scenario, such as one in which they are aware of all of the pertinent facts, and are unaware of their own position in society? For reasons of space I will not explore this further here, noting not only that *if* one finds the consent idea attractive, it is attractive in considering smaller police harms, but also that it is difficult to motivate it as providing an explanation of when larger police harms are justified.[30]

For the instrumental view, by appealing to simple consequentialist ideas, the setbacks imposed in the course of undercover work are justified if and only if they are straightforwardly outweighed by its benefits. This position is unattractive because it can be too relaxed about intruding upon or harming those who are known to be innocent. The dirty hands view, on the other hand, removes none of our anxiety about the apparent wrongs of undercover policing. The consent view is attractive but not sufficiently directive: it does not fully explain what we should or can legitimately consent to, and so leads us back towards where we started. In the next two chapters I set out a position that combines elements of all of the views canvassed here.

Notes

1 This usage mirror's W. D. Ross' concept of *prima facie* duties, which Ross characterises as 'conditional' duties. (Ross, W. D. The Right and the Good. Oxford: Oxford University Press, 2003 [1930], p. 19).

2 For a note on the distinction between *prima facie* and *pro tanto*, see Reisner, A. E. Prima Facie and Pro Tanto Oughts. International Encyclopedia of Ethics. Oxford: Blackwell, 2013.

3 Police Spies Out of Lives. 'Belinda's Story: As Told in Parliament'. https://policespiesoutoflives.org.uk/our-stories/belindas-story/belindas-story-audio/.

4 Marmor, Andrei. 'What Is the Right to Privacy?' Philosophy & Public Affairs 43, no. 1 (1 January 2015): 3–26. https://doi.org/10.1111/papa.12040.

5 Rachels, James. 'Why Privacy Is Important'. Philosophy and Public Affairs 4, no. 4 (1975): 323–33.
6 It is common to talk of 'harms' rather than 'impositions of setbacks of interests'. However, in a context in which we are discussing some of the relatively small individual effects that are caused by many intrusions, it is misleading to insinuate the permanence that is carried by the term 'harm'.
7 Joh, Elizabeth E., and Thomas Wuil Joo. 'Sting Victims: Third-Party Harms in Undercover Police Operations'. Southern California Law Review 88 (2015).
8 Marx, Gary T. 'Who Really Gets Stung? Some Issues Raised by the New Police Undercover Work'. Crime & Delinquency 28, no. 2 (1982): 165–93, p. 182.
9 Griffin, Nathan Stephens. '"Everyone Was Questioning Everything": Understanding the Derailing Impact of Undercover Policing on the Lives of UK Environmentalists'. Social Movement Studies (5 June 2020).
10 For a comprehensive critique of the slogan, see Solove, Daniel J. Nothing to Hide: The False Tradeoff between Privacy and Security. New Haven, CO: Yale University Press, 2011.
11 Special Demonstration Squad. 'Tradecraft Manual'. www.ucpi.org.uk/wp-content/uploads/2018/03/20180319-TC-DocumentsFinalVersion.pdf:

> the aspiring SOS officer's first major task on joining the back office was to spend hours and hours at St Catherine's House leafing through death registers in search of a name he could call his own. On finding a suitable ex-person, usually a deceased child or young person with a fairly anonymous name, the circumstances of his (or her) untimely demise was investigated. If the death was natural or otherwise unspectacular, and therefore unlikely to be findable in newspapers or other public records, the SDS officer would apply for a copy [of] the dead person's birth certificate. Further research would follow to establish the respiratory status of the dead person's family, if any, and, if they were still breathing, where they were living. If all was suitably obscure and there was little chance of the SOS officer or, more importantly, one of the wearies running into the dead person's parents/siblings etc., the SOS officer would assume squatters' rights over the unfortunate's identity for the next four years'.

12 Finckenauer, James. 'Organized Crime'. In The Oxford Handbook of Crime and Public Policy, 2008, p. 313.
13 Carter, Joe. Undercover. London: Arrow Books, 2017.
14 Dees, Tim. 'Here's the Hardest Part about Being an Undercover Cop'. Business Insider, 30 April 2014.
15 Consider the mixed report from the memoir Marcus, Tom. Soldier Spy. London: Penguin Books, 2016.

16 For Klockars, policing in general 'often' has this feature. Klockars, Carl B. 'The Dirty Harry Problem'. The Annals of the American Academy of Political and Social Science 452, no. 1 (1980): 33–47.

17 Marx, Gary T. Undercover: Police Surveillance in America. Berkeley: University of California Press, 1988, p. 96.

18 Expressing the inherent immorality, Skolnick holds both that: "Deception is considered by police – and courts as well – to be as natural as pouncing is to a cat." Skolnick, Jerome H. 'Deception by Police'. Criminal Justice Ethics 1, no. 2 (1982): 40–54, p. 40. And also: "in a moral society, authorities such as police would not be permitted to employ tactics that are generally regarded as immoral against those suspected, or accused, of a crime.(ibid., p. 52).

19 I use the terms incommensurable, incomparable, and incommensurate interchangeably. To be sure, some make distinctions between them.

20 This could also be labelled the 'consequentialist' view.

21 Hayden, Michael. 'Keynote Address: Cybersurveillance in the Post-Snowden Age', 2015. www.lawfareblog.com/lawfare-podcast-episode-108-general-michael-hayden-cybersurveillance-post-snowden-age at 13:10.

22 Saunders, Frances Stonor. 'Stuck on the Flypaper'. Otsuka Review of Books, 9 April 2015. David Cornwell, of course, went by the name John le Carré as a writer of fiction.

23 Mueller, John, and Mark G. Stewart. Terrorism, Security, and Money: Balancing the Risks, Benefits, and Costs of Homeland Security. Oxford and New York: Oxford University Press, 2011; Mueller, John E., and Mark G. Stewart. Chasing Ghosts. Oxford: Oxford University Press, 2015.

24 Marx, Gary T. 'Under-the-Covers Undercover Investigations: Some Reflections on the State's Use of Sex and Deception in Law Enforcement'. Criminal Justice Ethics 11, no. 1 (1 January 1992): 13–24, p. 18.

25 Lewis, Paul, and Rob Evans. Undercover: The True Story of Britain's Secret Police. London: Guardian Faber Publishing, 2014. See also the ongoing release of evidence in the Undercover Policing Inquiry www.ucpi.org.uk/published-evidence/

26 Walker, Clive, and Kingsley Hyland. 'Undercover Policing and Underwhelming Laws'. Criminal Law Review, no. 8 (21 March 2014): 572.

27 I return to the issue of compensation in chapter 4.

28 For more on this idea, see Baron, Marcia. 'The Mens Rea and Moral Status of Manipulation'. In Manipulation, edited by Christian Coons and Michael Weber. Oxford: Oxford University Press, 2014, pp. 118–20.

29 Hume, David. 'Of the Original Contract' in Essays: Moral, Political, and Literary (ed. Eugene Miller) Indianapolis: Liberty Fund (1985).

30 I return to policing by consent in ch.4§6, in discussing policing and democracy.

3   The liability view

1   The liability view

I turn to an explanation and defence of my preferred view of the normative status of undercover police work. The position I defend is called the liability view. According to this position, people can make themselves morally liable to the kinds of setback that are involved in being targeted by undercover police. For example, by participating in online groups that disseminate images of child sexual abuse, a person may make himself liable to being befriended and manipulated by an undercover officer in a way that permits the entire group to be dismantled. A complaint made by this target about his treatment intuitively carries no weight at all. Compare this with the complaint made by an innocent person who is intruded upon in a small way by undercover police, but in a manner that has overwhelming beneficial consequences. For example, consider the intrusions that undercover officers may impose upon the innocent associate of a person suspected of serious crime, simply in maintaining their cover. In that latter case, we do give weight to the complaint of the intruded-upon, even if we may consider that this complaint is ultimately outbalanced.

This chapter develops the position by drawing upon recent literature on the philosophy of self-defence. After developing that comparison, I show how considerations of proportionality, imperfect knowledge, and necessity apply in undercover policing. I also discuss how the view can account for the idea that those subject to undercover policing often are not objective threats, since police have either neutralised the threat or the investigation is backwards-looking.

DOI: 10.4324/9780429293443-3

While personal self-defence cases are typically drawn up with an attacker who threatens to kill a victim, and consider the ethics of killing the attacker, in our policing case, we are dealing with harms that are lesser and more complicated, including those associated with manipulation, deception, and intrusion. A goal of this book is to show how the self-defence framework can be usefully extended and illuminated by such an extension. With the same basic building blocks – liability, *pro tanto* wrongs, proportionality, and so forth – we can build a powerful model of the ethics of undercover policing.[1]

According to a natural viewpoint, we should have little sympathy for the complaints of those whose interests are set back by proportionate covert policing, where they are correctly suspected of involvement in crime. How can we account for this? It seems to be a case of a forfeiture of rights. The criminal's wrongful plans and behaviours cancel the moral complaint he would otherwise have. We can theorise this view by appeal to the principles that arise from considerations of personal self-defence. These cases provide a useful guide for our intuition, since they are structurally similar; they are also cases of rights-forfeiture.

Distinguish between an infringement and violation of a right. A 'rights violation' is a rights infringement that is not justified. A 'rights infringement' engages a right and gives rise to a complaint but may on balance be justified.[2] In a paradigm case of self-defence, one is morally permitted to use force in order to overcome a culpable threat. In so doing, one does not infringe upon the rights of one's attacker. Rather, by culpably creating the threat, the attacker forgoes his right not to be harmed. In the case of an innocent threat, we respond differently. Suppose someone will harm you through no fault of her own – she is going to fall onto you – and you can divert her body away from you, thereby harming her and saving yourself. In that case, it seems that by defending yourself, you (arguably justifiably) infringe upon the rights of the innocent threat. The culpable attacker, on the other hand, by creating a threat, loses a right not to be harmed. This is not just because by harming one's attacker, one saves oneself, but because of the attacker's responsibility for creating the threat.

The intuition that guides these cases also appears to be at work in cases of manipulative or deceptive police investigation. The man who takes part in a ring that distributes images of child sexual abuse makes himself liable to kinds of state action that set back his interests. These actions include his being systematically tricked, so that he reveals facts about himself and those using the ring. In taking part in the ring, he forgoes a number of rights, including his right against being deceived and manipulated. The harm that this person has unleashed is something that can be prevented or mitigated partly through means that impose direct costs upon him. He is morally culpable for a threat in the sense that he is responsible for a possible harm; his actions render him liable to being used as a means to the end of preventing or mitigating that harm.

Compare that case to the known-innocent subject of useful manipulation. Sometimes it will be useful for covert police to have effects upon those who are uninvolved in any criminal wrongdoing. For example, police may manipulate members of the family, sexual partners, or travel agent of their primary targets. Suppose that the manipulation is small and the security benefit is great. If such practices are ever on balance justified, many will still sense that those on the receiving end have their rights infringed. This contrasts with our sense that the culpable have no complaint at all.[3]

The view has the benefit over the positions canvassed in Chapter 2 that it tracks the intuition that some complaints against intrusive policing are cancelled by a person's actions. In self-defence, *moral responsibility for a threat* is sufficient for liability to harmful preventive action.[4] In policing, those who *culpably threaten criminality* similarly forfeit some rights against harm that they previously possessed. Similarly, in the area of punishment, Christopher Heath Wellman defends 'the rights forfeiture theory of punishment', which is 'the view that we should concentrate on which rights wrongdoers forfeit because this forfeiture is necessary and sufficient to explain the permissibility of punishment'.[5] Extending this to legitimate police action, we might say that threatened criminal activity is necessary and sufficient to explain liability to harmful police actions.[6]

2   Proportionality

Proportionality constraints apply in self-defence cases. Unlike aesthetic conceptions of proportionately, ethical proportionality describes limits. We do not say that an act is disproportionate if it involves less harm than the proportionality constraint describes. Ethical proportionality involves not going too far. Suppose B threatens only a minor violation of A's personal space: B threatens to step on A's foot. In this case, it is not permissible for A to shoot B dead as a preventive measure, even if this is the only way to avoid the threat. Similarly, ethical proportionality considerations apply in policing. The recent activities of police officers in infiltrating UK protest groups appear to the general public disproportionate – especially in going to the extreme depths of deception involved in having and raising children with their targets. In these cases, the harm to be prevented was direct public protest action. Is this undercover action a proportionate measure against a group whose most clear plan is to close down a power station for a week, with the goal of seeking media attention on environmental issues? Many would think not.

How much harm is it proportionate to use in fending off a threat? It appears that, across the scale of harms, it is permissible to impose a greater harm than that which is threatened. It is permissible to kill in self-defence against the person who threatens to seriously assault but not kill you.[7] If so, we can expect that police may similarly cause greater harm to those they pursue than the harm they are seeking to prevent.

We can distinguish between the following two conceptions of proportionality:

> *Narrow proportionality.* Weighing good effects against harms to the liable.
> *All-things-considered proportionality.* Weighing good effects against harms to both the liable and the non-liable.

The difference between the two is illustrated in the following example. Imagine a proposed operation to deploy undercover officers in an effort to infiltrate a fascistic organisation. The leaders of the group have been directly responsible for violence themselves and for organising and facilitating a great deal more violence. On examining the way that the operation is set up, it is noted that the focus is to be on gaining the trust of the organisation's leaders by covertly taking control of the organisation's leader's Sunday football league, his local pub, and his church. This operation might be narrowly proportionate but all-things-considered disproportionate. It is not disproportionate in the sense that the main target, given his actions, is liable to the actions of the officers. He has no legitimate complaint. But the operation is disproportionate in the sense that the effects on those targeted in the various surrounding social groupings are not liable, and are treated in a way that is, we may suppose, not justified by a preponderance of good consequences.

In the literature on self-defence and just war, it is common, drawing on the work of Jeff McMahan, to appeal to a concept of 'wide proportionality'.[8] This involves weighing good effects against harms to the non-liable. This concept is unhelpful for our present purposes for an interesting reason. The reason is that wide proportionality does not incorporate narrow proportionality. It is possible for an action to be narrowly disproportionate but widely proportionate, where a person is liable to harm x but has imposed upon her harm x+1, and where the latter is justified by the weight of good consequences. In discussions of war, this kind of case will get less attention because the harms under consideration are death and mutilation, and there is relatively little to add to these. In our context, however, this kind of case is likely to be very common, since there will be many cases of harms far less than death and mutilation, such as manipulation, time-wasting, and so forth. Here, it is confusing to have a concept labelled 'wide' that does not incorporate instances of our concept labelled 'narrow', and it is relevant to distinguish the narrow case from the all-things-considered case.[9]

Rønn and Lippert-Rasmussen argue that it makes an important difference to proportionality not just whether or how far the target is liable but also whether the intrusion is directly intended or merely foreseen.[10] On their view, there is a lesser burden of justification where the subject is liable, or where the intrusion is foreseen but unintended. Put another way, other things being equal, in order for an intervention to be proportionate, the benefits will need to be higher or the costs lower if the subject is liable, or if the intrusion is intended. Compare the following two cases illustrating harms upon the non-liable.

> Undercover 1. The surveillance or befriending by an undercover officer of the lover of the main target with a view to obtaining information about the target's whereabouts or finances.
> Undercover 2. An undercover officer befriends the main target, and as a foreseeable but unintended consequence befriends and thereby forms manipulative relationships with the main target's friends.

In the first case, the officer goes through the partner in order to get information about the target. In the second, the UC goes straight to the target and inflicts harms upon the others as a consequence. Consider a similar pair of cases concerning surveillance:

> Surveillance 1. Large amounts of information that is of 'no interested to an intelligence agency' is collected as a side-effect of its surveillance programme.
> Surveillance 2. A surveillance programme collects data from the same number of people 'with the aim of gaining information about some of the factors potentially leading to radicalized behavior'.[11]

In Undercover 1 and Surveillance 1, we have officers imposing setbacks upon the non-liable as foreseen but unintended consequences of their actions; in Undercover 2 and Surveillance 2, the setbacks are directly intended. If the harms and numbers of individuals are equivalent in each case, it seems intuitive, assert Rønn and Lippert-Rasmussen, that there is a range in which we would deem as proportionate interventions in Undercover 2 and Surveillance 2, but not Undercover 1 and Surveillance 1.

However, these examples are muddied because intended intrusions and manipulations tend to carry greater harms. The manipulation involved in getting a person to make an introduction to some other predetermined individual is greater than the manipulation involved in merely making small talk with a target's friends. Similarly, in the Surveillance cases, it can be expected that the information will be analysed and acted upon in the second but not the first surveillance case, and this is a greater harm. What seems to make the main difference is not the different intention, but the greater intrusion. Unlike in discussions of war, where some civilian deaths from bombings may be understood as foreseen but unintended, in the investigative context, intended harms will be sustained and forceful and carry greater analysis and action, and the harm lies in these activities.

There does at first seem to be a difference between, on one hand, an undercover officer actively deceiving and manipulating the innocent associate of a target so that he can gain access to the target, and, on the other hand, foreseeably but unintentionally deceiving and manipulating the innocent associate so that the officer's cover will be retained. It is difficult in practice to credit the idea that direct deception and manipulation by an officer is *unintended*, even if the officer would not have sought the person out: there is still the calculation of the person's beliefs, an assessment of what actions it will take to be plausible, to ensure that they take the conversation in the right direction, and so forth.

There is, however, a category of harms that are relevant to this point. These are the indirect harms described in Chapter 2: financial effects on third parties, undesirable chilling effects, harms to officers, effects on trust in institutions. In the fake fence case, the financial effects on local businesses are good examples of foreseen but unintended harms. These are clearly unrelated and of no potential use to the agents. These remain serious and real harms. Nonetheless, if it is right that foreseen but unintended harms are easier to justify, then these kinds of harms receive less weight in a judgment of all-things-considered proportionality.

When undercover officers manipulate, they might be construed as doing so as a foreseen but unintended consequence of their action, but the nature of manipulation makes this an awkward construction. Manipulation just does involve treating another as a means to some other end. Is it more permissible to treat someone as a means to an end if I am treating them as a means to an end as a means to another end, rather than treating them as a means to an end in themselves? Surely not. The financial effects on the local business may, then, be easier to justify because they are not intended. Other aspects of undercover work are inherently exploitative, even when they are justified.

3   Imperfect knowledge

Clearly, police do not always have knowledge of people's involvement in crime before they carry out an operation. One of the functions of an operation is precisely to obtain that knowledge.[12] Does this provide an objection to my claim that some can be liable to intrusions? It might seem to place the police in a morally impossible situation, in which the legitimacy of their actions is dependent upon knowledge that they can only acquire in the process of acting.

We are used to the idea of moral uncertainty in other areas of life. Such uncertainty comes in degrees. By switching on a light, I have a reasonable belief that I am going to illuminate the room. Unknown to me, the switch has maliciously been wired so that it ignites a fuse on an explosive. I am not at all culpable for the results of my switching on the light. From a fact-relative perspective, I have caused an explosion that has harmed innocents, and it is wrong, absent some special justification, to harm innocents. But the fact-relative perspective is inaccessible to me. Or insofar as it is accessible – I might hereafter examine closely any switch before pressing it – I can only access it by performing other actions that may similarly carry a fact-relative wrong. A new situation may be configured such that acts of examining a switches will ignite some unknown explosive, or such that failing to turn a switch when expected will cause the ignition. Clearly, wrongs must be judged from some belief-relative perspective. The purely fact-relative perspective does not track our everyday assessments of people's actions, it makes extreme demands on action (and inaction), and the demands are so extreme and contradictory that they may in principle be impossible to meet, with the result that moral principles can only provide *post facto* assessments but can no longer guide action.

In this spirit, Derek Parfit writes, 'We cannot base our decisions on the facts except by basing our decisions on what we now believe to be the facts.'[13] That is, right action may be belief relative rather than fact relative. Where police have strong reason to believe that a person is involved in crime, and there is a way to prevent that crime that, with a very high probability, will impose small setback upon that person, then – on the assumption that police acted in accordance with proper procedure – it is difficult to claim that police acted *wrongly* by acting to prevent the crime, even where it turns out that the person was in fact innocent.

However, right action cannot be purely belief-relative. We do hold people responsible for the steps that they take to acquire knowledge. Imagine that, having taken heed of the idea that norms are not purely fact-relative, I minimise what I can learn about my surroundings, and cause a harm that I did not know would occur, but that any observer would judge that I ought to have expected. Imagine a target's suspicious and unstable behaviour is easily discoverable on social media. Police target this person with an undercover officer without making this check, and the deployment ends up in violence. If police shirk seeking out the evidence on which they should base their investigations, it is not an excuse for them to say that they acted properly in accordance with the beliefs that they had. Right action seems, then, to be relative to the beliefs that one *ought* to have against the constraints one faces in fact. One ought to take reasonable efforts to understand the circumstances of one's action, and it is possible to act wrongfully in wilful or negligent ignorance. Conversely, it is possible to act justifiably in carrying out an action that is wrongful from an omniscient point of view, where the facts cannot reasonably be accessed.

Apart from being culpable for a threat, one can also become liable to defensive force by being culpable for causing people to believe that one is a threat. Suppose that as part of a provocative conceptual art project someone dresses up as a bank robber, withdraws some of his own cash from the bank desk, and dashes out of the building with the money in a sack labelled 'swag'.[14] This may warrant some police attention. The analogy to self-defence is now helpful. This case is equivalent to one in which a person performs acts that create the impression of a threat, even when there is none. In both cases, it will be a matter of degree and context how far we deem the act wrong in itself as a needless creation of fear and disruption, and how far we deem it a humorous poke at a culture of excessive security. In neither case is the person culpable *for a threat*. Now suppose police deploy intrusive methods upon the joke bank robber on the grounds of the reasonable suspicion that he created. That is a case that we judge differently to one in which a target becomes subject to reasonable but mistaken suspicion through no fault of her own.

I return to this topic in Chapter 4.

4   Necessity

It is a widespread position reflected not only in philosophical work but also in the law, especially international law, that a principle of necessity applies to justified self-defence. In general, the principle of necessity states that one can impose only the degree of harm that is necessary to prevent the harm with which one is threatened. Consider two cases. In the first, one is threatened with a serious harm and can prevent this harm only by killing one's assailant. In the second case, one is threatened with the same harm, and one can prevent this harm by either killing one's assailant or fleeing. In both cases, killing seems to be a proportionate response, but in the second case, it is not necessary. It appears that considerations of proportionality ask us to compare the value gained against the disvalue imposed, whereas considerations of necessity ask us to compare the disvalue imposed against the disvalue that could be imposed by taking a different course of action that achieves the same value.

Similarly, a deployment of a group undercover agents to infiltrate a violent political group may be proportionate, in that it prevents a concerted series of terrorist actions, but unnecessary, if the disruption of the group could be achieved with the use of surveillance, which, we can assume at least in this case, involves less intrusion, manipulation, deception, direct harms, and harms to officers. Conversely, a deployment may be necessary but disproportionate, as where undercover officers are deployed with the goal of ensuring that parents do not lie about their addresses on application forms for their children's schools, or where political groups that aim at nothing more criminal than aggravated trespass are heavily infiltrated.[15] We may assume that the value in these cases – compliance with school catchment rules, the integrity of land and property ownership – could not be achieved with the use of less intrusive means than undercover policing but also that the value gained is out of proportion to the costs imposed.

Undercover police, and those authorising them, will, of course, very often lack knowledge of whether the harms and setbacks that they impose are necessary or not. The point of much undercover work is to gain an understanding of an organisation and its accompanying threats. In order to have a claim to knowledge of whether there is another way of preventing a threatened harm – or indeed, the extent and nature of the threatened harm – it may be necessary to perform undercover work and to impose some of the harms that it carries. It thus becomes, *ex ante*, impossible for police to apply the principle of necessity that applies in personal self-defence cases, since that principle is designed for cases in which the agent has knowledge of the immediate threat. Does this amount to a problem for the liability view, or the necessity principle?

If it is a problem for the liability view, then it renders much undercover policing impossible to carry out legitimately. However, I suggest we should instead revise our understanding of the necessity principle. The principle of necessity is difficult to interpret when uncertainty is introduced. Suppose we can avert a national security threat by (a) using a method that has a 0.5 chance of success and will not intrude in the private affairs of others, or (b) a 0.9 chance of success and will intrude significantly in the private affairs of others.[16] Is the second method necessary to stop the threat?

Suppose we understand right action as relative to beliefs that one ought reasonably to hold (as I suggest earlier). In this case, the necessity principle is indeterminate: it stays silent on matters of probability. Alternatively, suppose that the necessity principle applies in a fact relative way, whereby one ought to act in a way that in fact is necessary to prevent the harm, even if one can only possibly know, *ex post*, whether a less harmful course of action would have avoided the harm. In this case, the necessity principle is implausibly stringent, assigning wrongful action on the basis of epistemically inaccessible counterfactuals.

It is commonplace in both law and security ethics to state the principle without discussion of such complexities. As we have just seen, it is misleading to do so. For example, David Omand asserts that, in intelligence matters, methods must be applied 'intruding no more than necessary into the private affairs of others'.[17] Necessity conditions stated in this way fail to take account of uncertainty about success. While credible and potentially crucial as regulatory rules of thumb, I suggest that we would do well here to place our focus on proportionality, and incorporate into that concept the important idea that the necessity principle contains, namely, that assessments of harmful actions should take account not only of the benefits that are produced but also of the other ways that those benefits could have been produced.

Policing contexts of designing undercover operations do not typically possess the urgency of personal self-defence cases. In self-defence cases, a key issue is whether the attacker is (or would be) culpable for the harm that would occur, were no defensive intervention to take place. Paradigm cases involve waiting until the attack is imminent. Preemptive strikes are difficult to justify. Police interventions, on the other hand, take place in slower motion. The immediacy is not present. An express goal of covert police work is to facilitate an intervention well before a threatened criminal harm occurs. This might be thought to provide a relevant difference between the moralities of personal self-defence and policing.

Nonetheless, consider why there is the need for immediacy in cases of legitimate personal self-defence. I propose the following. Before the attack is imminent, it is typically not the case that it can be established with sufficient certainty that self-defensive force is necessary in order to avert the threat. Thus, the central objection to preemptive strikes is that there is typically too high a chance that the subject of the attack would not in fact have made an attack. The preemptive strike is thereby typically better understood as a case of aggression. However, where there is an extremely high degree of certainty that an attack is imminent, and that a forceful response is the only viable effective form of defence, we jettison the notion that preemptive strikes are acts of aggression and instead classify them as self-defence.

In the case of policing, where the information-attaining power of the state is at work, things are different to the case of war. Police can be aware with high certainty that an individual threatens a harm far in advance of his placing his finger on a trigger. The point about urgency, then, does not undermine the analogy to self-defence cases. Instead it leads us to probe more deeply what lessons we can draw from it. Imminence as urgency plays an evidentiary role, indicating threathood, and it is sufficient certainty of threathood, and of the necessity of defensive force, that changes the moral landscape.

My claim, then, is that the most persuasive reason for it being a necessary condition of legitimate self-defence that the threat is immediate is that only immediate threats are typically known of with certainty. Police can often know with certainty of the existence of a threat and its surrounding circumstances before it is immediate.

5 The scope of 'threat'

If a person is, or would be, culpable for a possible harm, then she forgoes a right against harmful intervention. We can understand the referent of 'harm' so that it is the exact harm that would occur, were preventive force not to be used. This gives rise to a possible disanalogy between policing and personal self-defensive cases. From a certain perspective, someone who offers to sell contraband to a police officer who is acting undercover threatens no harm at all. If the sale goes ahead, the goods will be destroyed. It seems that the right comparison is not with a pure case of personal self-defence. In those cases, if the attacker is not deflected, a harm occurs. The right comparison appears to be to an attacker who, unknown to him, has been rendered safe. Suppose that his gun was emptied of bullets earlier by the person who is to be threatened. Just as the sale of contraband to police will not involve the distribution of goods into the wrong hands, so the unwittingly disarmed attacker will be unable to cause a harm if he pulls his trigger. Is it permissible to harm the unwittingly disarmed in order to prevent him from carrying out what he wrongly believes would be a harmful attack? The intuitive answer is 'no'. After all, what good comes of this harm? By hypothesis, if he pulls his trigger, nothing will happen. But what police do when they carry out a sting is equivalent to harming an unwittingly disarmed attacker. Does that mean that police stings are impermissible – or is there a morally relevant disanalogy between stings and harm to attackers who cannot succeed?

One response would be to subjectivise fully the understanding of harm. On this view, if someone is culpable for what she believes is a possible harm, then she forgoes a right against intervention. This would retain the analogy between the sting and the self-defence case but deny the intuition that we cannot harm the disarmed attacker.

That intuition is difficult to abandon. We can do better than that. Policing and personal self-defence cases have an important similarity, which is that it is difficult to describe instances of genuinely harmless unwittingly disarmed attackers. Those whose attacks fail by one means are likely to find others. And those whose sales of contraband fail by one means are likely to find others. Someone who sells illicit goods to a police officer who is acting undercover also threatens to perform the same harm in selling such goods to those who would use them. We would do better to understand the threatened harm in this case to be wider than just the imminent harm of selling the goods involved in the sting but also the implied threat to continue to deal in contraband. If so, the police operation can, after all, be morally comparable to a case of self-defence. It is an intervention at a non-imminent stage of the threat.

How do we deal with intrusions and manipulations where a target's plans and activities are not criminal at all, including any inchoate offence? Consider, for example, the recent case in which a paid informant for the New York Police Department's intelligence unit was under orders to 'bait' Muslims into making remarks in favour of terrorism.[18] Leaving aside for the moment the issues of entrapment, to which I return later, and assuming for the sake of argument that the strategy has some security value, it is relevant here that manipulations were visited upon those not suspected of posing any threat. The liability view handles this case well. Police involvement where there is not yet a crime, even an inchoate crime, is comparable to self-defence where there is not yet a threat, but only a possible future threat. Culpability on the part of the purported future threat is absent and such cases thereby fall under the heading of intrusions that must be justified by the high bar of a preponderance of good consequences, analogous to harming the innocent bystander in exchange for a significant benefit.[19]

A related question is how we understand the relation between threat and liability. That is, are people liable to harmful undercover policing only for operations that are aimed at preventing the *specific* threats that they pose? Or, can people be so liable in virtue of posing a certain kind of threat? The intuitive answer is that the connection between the threat and the liability is close. Suppose the leader of a religious group is committing serious fraud for personal gain. Does he thereby make himself liable to heavy manipulation as part of an undercover operation aimed at infiltrating a group that seeks to commit terrorist acts? Perhaps not. In personal self-defence, people forgo rights against harm in virtue of and in the context of a threat that they create; people do not forgo all of their rights against harm when they commit any wrong.[20]

6 Backwards-looking policing

In working from principles of self-defence, it appears that we are able to only consider possible future harms. The self-defence model involves a potential harm that can be prevented. An individual who has previously carried out some unjust threat, and no longer poses a further threat, does not call for defensive action. This points us towards the conclusion that policing, as understood through the lens of the liability model, should be prepared to make greater intrusions in preventing criminal acts, than they would be in pursuing criminals for prosecution, where there is reason to believe that the person is unlikely to reoffend.[21]

Consider the case of Keith Hall, whose wife had disappeared in a way that raised police suspicions, partly because her bank account was left unused and she had just met with a lawyer seeking a divorce:

> [Police] were about to give up on the investigation when they had a call from a woman who had put an ad in the lonely hearts section of the local paper. One of the replies was from Keith Hall. She wanted police advice: was it safe to meet him? The police said it was not – they would deal with replying to Hall.
>
> Jim Bancroft, the detective leading the investigation, saw a golden opportunity to introduce an undercover officer to Keith Hall. The officer chosen for the job was a tall, good-looking woman who was also named 'Liz'.
>
> Hall seems to have been bowled over by her from the moment they met. He wined and dined her, and gave her gifts. . . . Finally, he proposed marriage.
>
> 'Liz' replied that she could not marry him because his wife might come back and 'ruin everything'. He said that wouldn't happen. She said he could not be sure. He insisted that he could be sure, and then explained why: 'I strangled her', he sobbed. 'But it wasn't that easy . . . I didn't plan nothing . . . I just did it'.
>
> And what did you do with the body, 'Liz' asked calmly. 'Put it in an incinerator', Hall explained.
>
> The police had taped the whole conversation.[22]

In practice, the distinction between investigating the threatened and the unpunished crime will often be invisible. That an individual has committed a crime and has faced no reprimand is some evidence that he will commit further crimes.[23] Nonetheless, the liability view appears to imply that a credibly repentant unpunished elderly war criminal is liable to less intrusion than a conspiring war-criminal-to-be. That is not counterintuitive. The view has that implication because the threat involved in conspiring to commit serious crimes renders a person liable to heavy preventive measures.

The liability view has a related possible implication that may be counterintuitive. This is the implication that the credibly repentant criminal is liable to the same level of intrusion as the pure innocent and indeed has the same rights of resistance and compensation. The liability model seems to imply this because both the innocent and the reformed but unpunished criminal are equally non-threats. Is it ever permissible for undercover police to deploy with an entirely retrospective outlook? The liability model seems to give a presumption against this.

I would respond, however, that this is implication is not as counterintuitive as it appears. *Purely* retrospective deployments of undercover police will seem wasteful, at best, where the opportunity cost involves harm prevention. Further, the repentant criminal may be responsible for the threatened harms of others, even if he is not involved in them now. Suppose the police are investigating threatened crimes by fascist groups. The repentant war criminal may bear responsibility for inciting those groups, and thereby become liable to intrusions.

Alternatively, some might take the view that the facilitation of retribution is an important function of police, and that where an investigation is likely both to prevent harm *and* to ensure that a person who has committed a serious wrong will be punished, there is extra reason to pursue it, in comparison to an investigation that will *merely* prevent harm. Can this retributivist view be accommodated? An argument that does so is the following.[24] Those who create a threat but are thereafter bystanders are liable to defensive harm in a way that pure bystanders are not. For example, suppose that, in defending yourself against a bomb that cannot be defused, you can choose to throw either the person who set the explosives in the way of the blast, or an innocent. It seems that you should use the person who set the explosives. People can be liable to such 'opportunistic' harm if they are responsible for the threat. The person who creates the threat incurs this liability because he has a duty to avert it. He may *also* have a duty to avert other threats to the victim, particularly if he is unable to avert this particular threat. If one way of discharging that latter duty is through the general deterrence effect of punishment, then police will be warranted in using harmful methods, including deceptive and manipulative methods, for the purposes of facilitating the courts in bringing people to judgment, even where they do not pose an immediate threat of harm. The elderly, credibly repentant war criminal has a duty to turn himself in and thereby contribute to the deterrence of future possible war criminals; his failure to carry out this duty renders him liable to the kinds of setbacks that police impose in carrying out their investigations, including the setbacks associated with undercover policing.

Return to the case of Keith Hall, with which I opened this section. If Hall were innocent, even in the face of some evidence to the contrary prior to the undercover operation, then we would deem the operation to be quite wrongful because of the non-liability of the target. This illustrates the moral riskiness of the deployment and the workings of the liability idea. In the next chapter, I will explore further such risks under the heading of 'epistemically justified wrongs'.

In this section, we have seen how it seems that while personal self-defence is always forwards-looking in the sense that it is centrally concerned with possible future harms, undercover policing practice may in part have the function of facilitating recompense for past wrongs, of bringing people to justice. I reply by expressing scepticism about purely backwards-looking police work, and moreover by showing how the liability view might be extended to account for people's duties to provide recompense. It remains the case, then, that the analogy to personal self-defence provides a forceful guide to our norms in this area, and a framework that is superior to the dirty hands and simple consequentialist models that were mooted in Chapter 2.

7   Concluding note: extreme harms

The discussion illustrates the fruitfulness and power of the rights framework that has recently been applied to the ethics of personal self-defence and war. Unlike those applications, policing typically (but not always) involves the imposition of much lesser harms. The extension of the framework into policing is in one way natural: both war and policing involve state coercion. If we can deepen our understanding of the legitimacy of one kind of state violence by appeal to cases of the ethics of personal self-defence, we might expect to do so in other cases too. The contexts of war and policing are, however, in other ways very different. International law does not carry the force of domestic law, and the international laws of war are forged out of conditions of emergency and necessity, and against the context of widespread brutality. One should only read between the two with a great deal of caution. Doing so is not my project here. I am interested in the common ancestor of both approaches, which are the ideas of liability, rights forfeiture, and proportionality, especially as illustrated through hypothetical cases of personal self-defence.

Although the framework begins with individual ethics, policy considerations are never far away. Consider cases in which police cause extreme harms upon individual citizens as part of their operations: serious bodily harm, torture, death, assaults on sexual and reproductive integrity.

The recently declassified field guide for UK undercover operatives advises that sexual relations with targets should be avoided, but that where they are entered into, 'you should try to have a fleeting, disastrous relationships with individuals who are not important to your sources of information'.[25] In contrast, the Canadian system permits that officers can break the law if it is 'reasonable and proportional in the circumstances'. But it excludes actions that 'result in "death or bodily harm", constitute a violation of the "sexual integrity of an individual", or a "willful attempt" to obstruct justice'.[26]

There are those who argue that placing clear public rules on what an officer cannot do while undercover – such as taking drugs or having sexual relations with their targets – places limits on them that are often excessive. The argument holds that groups that are being infiltrated will have incentives to engineer situations in which the rules are tested.[27]

The framework that I defend in this book does not by itself rule any of these actions out as a matter of principle. It is unlikely that a person can make themselves liable to such extreme harms as carried out by police, as they can barely be made liable to any of them even in the stricter context of the courts. But it is possible in principle that overwhelming good consequences could make such actions justifiable in some circumstances. In the present political context, given scandals around excessive policing of protest groups and racism, such restrictions appear apposite. However, in a more ideal context, it is conceivable that the imposition of extreme harms upon individuals is justified in the manner of the ticking bomb scenario, in which a terrible harm to many citizens can only be avoided by imposing torture on one person.[28] Like that scenario, there are often reasons to doubt that the imposition of serious harm is the best course of action:[29] in the policing context, it is easy to understate the third-party and broader harms involved in undercover work, and it may be that tactics involving surveillance may not only be more expensive but also preferable. Further, there are costs to having institutions that can in principle carry out torture or other extreme harms, in particular, such structures are in tension with liberal values and this dissonance can be damaging to the way that our polity functions.[30] Finally, as with discussions of torture, we might countenance the possibility that the imposition by the state of extreme harms should never be legalised, for pragmatic reasons, even if it can conceivably be morally permissible.[31]

Notes

1 Coons and Webber note that such an extension has not yet been systematically put forward. Coons, Christian, and Michael Weber. 'The Ethics of Self-Defence: The Current Debate'. In The Ethics of Self-Defense. New York: Oxford University Press, 2016, fn.3.
2 Thomson, Judith Jarvis. 'Some Ruminations on Rights'. In Rights, Restitution, and Risk: Essays, in Moral Theory, edited by William Parent. Cambridge, MA: Harvard University Press, 1986, p. 51.
3 Other authors on police ethics allude to the idea of liability. John Kleinig writes: 'inhabitants of the world of criminal activity, a world that by definition relies on force and deception, must expect that force and deception will be used to counter them. Criminals can hardly express surprise if they are investigated by deceptive means' (The Ethics of Policing. Cambridge University Press, 1996, p. 133). He rightly retreats from that version of the view. It appears to have the implication that torturers and sexual abusers are liable to torture and sexual abuse by the police when those methods are deployed as preventive measures. He thus notes that '[m]eans are independently evaluable, and not just in relation to their ends'. (op. cit., p. 301n28). The evaluation of ends that he subsequently provides departs from the liability idea. Seumas Miller conceives of the police function as 'the protection of justifiably enforceable moral rights' (The Moral Foundations of Social Institutions: A Philosophical Study. Cambridge: Cambridge University Press, 2010, p. 262). He incorporates into his position the view that 'human rights . . . are justifiably enforceable; for example, A has a right not to be assaulted by B, and if B assaults or attempts to assault A, then B can legitimately be prevented from assaulting A by means of coercion' (op. cit., p. 247). Justifiably enforceable rights include human rights, and the 'enforcement' of a right can include the use of coercion. This would seem to suggest that those who act wrongly make themselves liable to harmful police action. Miller sums up his view as, 'harmful and normally immoral methods are on occasion necessary to realize the fundamental end of policing', offering several examples, including, 'a drug dealer might have to be deceived

if a drug ring is to be smashed, a blind eye might have to be turned to the minor illegal activity of an informant if the flow of important information he provides in relation to serious crimes is to continue' (op. cit., p. 264). Those cases are distinct in liability terms, where the first involves the deception of someone who is liable to such treatment, whereas the second involves harms to innocent victims of the informant's minor crimes. The work that I do here develops the insight by paying close attention to the nature and shape of liability to harmful police actions.

4 Some might argue that moral responsibility for a threat is not sufficient for harmful defensive action, since those who are responsible for a threat but do not constitute it are not liable. The distinction does not affect the argument here. Furthermore, in chapter 4 I look also further at necessary conditions for liability.

5 Wellman, Christopher Heath. 'The Rights Forfeiture Theory of Punishment'. Ethics 122, no. 2 (1 January 2012): 371–93, p. 375.

6 There are three points to note about this position, concerning in particular the claim that threatened criminality is a necessary condition for liability to police intrusion. First, in chapter 4 I will examine an argument that innocent associates of criminal targets may be liable to intrusions. We will see how involvement in criminality or a public wrong is sufficient but not necessary for liability. Second, as discussed in chapter 2, people may be liable to less harmful intrusions because they are consented-to. Third, the principle refers to threatened criminality: to public wrongs. Some wrongs, including seriously harmful wrongs, are private. People aren't liable to harmful intrusions in virtue of carrying out awful manipulations of their friends. This is an issue of police legitimacy: we retain rights of enforcement in those cases, rather than have police act on our behalf. We do not tend to think that bad people are liable to more aggressive police intrusions, if their badness manifests itself only in non-criminalisable wrongful acts.

7 Uniacke, Suzanne. 'Proportionality and Self-Defense'. Law and Philosophy 30, no. 3 (2011): 261.

8 McMahan, Jeff. Killing in War. Oxford: Oxford University Press, 2009.

9 McMahan states that he uses the terms 'wide' and 'narrow' because wide proportionality usually involves more people. (McMahan, Jeff. 'Proportionate Defense'. In Weighing Lives in War, edited by Jens David Ohlin, Larry May, and Claire Finkelstein. Oxford, UK: Oxford University Press, 2017.) This will not always be the case in undercover work, where there may be serious infringements of the privacy of a few non-liable actors at the periphery of a large organised crime group.

10 Rønn, Kira Vrist, and Kasper Lippert-Rasmussen. 'Out of Proportion? On Surveillance and the Proportionality Requirement'. Ethical Theory and Moral Practice 23, no. 1 (1 February 2020): 181–99.

11 Quoting from ibid., p. 191.

12 For a discussion of ethics and the intelligence ladder, see Bellaby, Ross W. The Ethics of Intelligence: A New Framework. Abingdon, UK: Routledge, 2014.

13 Parfit, Derek. On What Matters. Oxford: Oxford University Press, 2013, p. 162.

14 Thanks to Victor Tadros for pointing me to this real life example.

15 For an helpful explication of these categories and deployment of these examples, see Macnish, Kevin. The Ethics of Surveillance. Oxford: Routledge, 2017.

16 Lazar, Seth. 'Necessity in Self-Defense and War'. Philosophy & Public Affairs 40, no. 1 (2012): 3–44.

17 Omand, David. 'Ethical Guidelines in Using Secret Intelligence for Public Security'. Cambridge Review of International Affairs 19, no. 4 (2006): 613–28, p. 621. See also David Omand. Securing the State, Chapter 10.

18 Associated Press. 'Informant: NYPD Paid Me to "Bait" Muslims', October 2012. www.ap.org/Content/AP-In-The-News/2012/Informant -NYPD-paid-me-to-bait-Muslims (accessed May 2021).

19 I return to the idea of a preponderance of good consequences in chapter 4. Attempts in law are widely debated. See Duff, Antony. Criminal Attempts. Oxford and New York: Oxford University Press, 1997. See also Lippke, R. L. A Limited Defense of What Some Will Regard as Entrapment. Legal Theory 23, no. 4 (2017): 283–306, pp. 304ff.

20 Compare, however, Otsuka's argument that those convicted of crimes can have a higher tax rate imposed upon them (Otsuka, M. Libertarianism without Inequality. Oxford: Clarendon Press, 2003). Moreover, compare Tadros' argument that those who try to get away with crime have an undischarged obligation to make reparations, and the failure to meet that obligation makes it permissible to imprison them as a means to disincentivising other possible criminals (Tadros, V. The Ends of Harm: The Moral Foundations of Criminal Law. Oxford: Oxford University Press, 2011.) Both these are arguments for imposing upon on those who do wrong costs that are not immediately connected to the wrong that they have committed.

21 Clive Harfield argues that undercover policing in fact tends to be deployed with the goal of uncovering evidence about past crimes. 'Undercover Policing: A Legal-Comparative Perspective'. In Comparative Policing from a Legal Perspective, edited by Monica den Boer. Cheltenham: Edward Elgar Publishing, 2018, pp. 153–68.

22 Alasdair Palmer. 'Colin Stagg's Shadow Hangs over Undercover Police Work'. The Telegraph, 17 August 2008. The prosecution was unsuccessful because the undercover officer was deemed to have carried out an interview without due process. The trial judge made Hall's name public.

23 To be sure, that a person has committed a crime and has faced reprimand is also statistical evidence that he will commit another crime.

24 Drawing on Tadros, The Ends of Harm.

25 'Tradecraft: Binder 2', p. 28. www.ucpi.org.uk/wp-content/uploads/ 2018/03/20180319-TC-Documents*Final*Version.pdf (accessed November 2021). See also See Marx, Gary T. 'Under-the-Covers Undercover Investigations: Some Reflections on the State's Use of Sex and Deception in Law Enforcement'. Criminal Justice Ethics 11, no. 1 (1 January 1992): 13–24.

26 Joh, Elizabeth E. 'Breaking the Law to Enforce It: Undercover Police Participation in Crime'. Stanford Law Review 62 (2009): 181.

27 Anecdotally, police officers are divided on this issue. In any case, the recent Authorised Professional Practice document put in place by the College of Policing sets out a series of limits on police acting undercover.

28 There is a disanalogy, in that the victim of torture in the ticking bomb scenario is usually understood to be culpable for the bomb threat.

29 Shue, Henry. 'Torture in Dreamland: Disposing of the Ticking Bomb'. Case Western Reserve Journal of International Law 37 (2005): 231.

30 Waldron, Jeremy. 'Torture and Positive Law: Jurisprudence for the White House'. Columbia Law Review 105, no. 6 (2005): 1681–750.

31 McMahan, Jeff. 'Torture in Principle and in Practice'. Public Affairs Quarterly 22, no. 2 (2008): 111–28.

4 Weak links and justified wrongs

1 The fringes of criminal groups: liability without culpability

This chapter further explores the liability view and its implications, covering three topics of practical and philosophical importance. These topics all relate to the ideal of applying undercover policing in a proportionate manner, and are given their clearest expression in cases of targets who turn out to be innocent or only minimally culpable. The topics are (a) the exact form of responsibility that can give rise to liability; (b) on-balance justified undercover work that gives rise to legitimate complaints from the innocent or disproportionately intruded upon ('consequentially justified harms'); (c) those who are *ex post* seen to be wrongfully intruded upon even where there was *ex ante* reason to believe that there was moral liability ('epistemically justified wrongs'). My view has the implication that police can commit wrongs that are justified by epistemic or overwhelming consequentialist considerations. I therefore discuss reparations and the right to resist police wrongs.

Let us turn to the first of those topics. In order to establish himself as a credible member of a group, an undercover officer begins by befriending the partner of a friend of the main target. Such activity involves several of the setbacks described in Chapters 1 and 2: time and social capital is taken up by a personal relationship that has a hidden expiry date; the target is intruded upon and manipulated; and so forth. Is the partner any threat at all? Seemingly not. The setbacks imposed on her are purely instrumental. Her actions are separate from the crime that is being investigated. She appears

DOI: 10.4324/9780429293443-4

to be an innocent bystander. For example, infiltration of low level drug dealers – who may be better described as drug users who are exploited by an organised criminal group – can be the best way to gain access to higher level drug dealers. Although the immediate target is the low level dealer, the ultimate target is the higher level criminal organisation, and it is implicitly accepted that it would be disproportionate to deploy undercover officers if the low level dealer is acting in isolation (say, in independently producing drugs). The justification for the high level of intrusion that is involved in the undercover tactic refers to the broader range of wrongs committed by the criminal organisation: violence, fraud, dealing in weapons and other contraband, as well as the rationale of preventing the distribution of drugs.[1]

These kinds of cases, where we focus on the peripheries and associates of criminal organisations force us to examine more closely the liability view of intrusive policing. There are two separate issues that we need to address here. First, can those who are *not* responsible for a threat be liable to the setbacks of undercover police work? Second, can those who are *minimally* responsible for a threat associated with a criminal organisation be liable to significant setbacks associated with undercover police work? In this section I will explore the issue with respect to the non-responsible. In the following section I discuss the minimally responsible.

Where police impose serious setbacks upon those who are not responsible for a threat, we tend to say that those people were not liable. It may be the case that liability to lesser harms can be accounted for by appeal to consent. We saw, in Chapter 2, how smaller harms associated with policing may be understood as not wrongful, since people can be construed as having agreed to a chance of facing such harms. For example, an undercover officer goes into a shop with his target, and in doing so deceives and manipulates, in a relatively small way, those working in the shop.

Are there situations in which those who are not responsible for a criminal threat are liable to *greater* harms associated with undercover policing? Several writers in the self-defence literature think that there can be liability without culpability. For example, the driver of the out-of-control car may be liable to defensive harm where his vehicle can only be stopped by harming him. In this case, even though the driver is not morally responsible – he took reasonable precautions in maintaining his car and was simply unfortunate that it malfunctioned – liability arises because the driver is the agent of the harm.[2] Others hold that the innocent can be liable to defensive harm by posing a threat that would also violate a person's rights, even where *no* agency is involved on the part of the innocent in creating the threat.[3] Call this the 'unjust threat' view.

If liability arises there, it might similarly arise in the case of the innocent associate of the serious criminal. Such an associate might be understood to be liable to harmful action that will avert the threat of the criminal group. Many activities involve risks of imposing or facilitating a harm. As the head of an internet service provider, you risk hosting communications channels that are used for the purposes of paedophile groups. This risk will generate some duty to cooperate with police. Furthermore, on the agency view, it may also make one liable to intrusive state activities, such as surveillance or 'equipment interference' (i.e. hacking), if those are among the most effective ways of mitigating the threat. Similarly, on the agency and unjust threat views, if one takes part in a political group that has a hidden violent wing, one may thereby become liable to a degree of manipulative infiltration tactics, even if the violent goals of the group are well-hidden, insofar as one (unknowingly) contributes to the threat. If the members of the family, the lover, or travel agent, of a serious criminal contribute to the threat he poses, then, on this position, they too make themselves liable to some preventive harm, even if this contribution is unintended and the criminality is hidden from their view.

There is a theoretical and a practical reason to think that those who are non-responsibly part of a threat can be liable to serious undercover police harms. The theoretical reason is that one difference between policing cases and personal self-defence cases is that, properly applied, the analogy in policing involves *other*-defence, not *self*-defence. It may, for example, be the case that (a) one can permissibly defend oneself against an innocent threat without bringing about better overall consequences and also that (b) one can only permissibly defend another person against an innocent threat if the consequences of doing so are overwhelmingly positive. The reason for the difference is that people have a prerogative to take extra account of their own interests, beyond what is warranted by an agent-neutral perspective.[4] Police, in contrast, should be neutral. They do not have reasons to prefer some citizens over others. This has an effect on the proportionality considerations. It means that, other things being equal, police face a higher bar of justification in imposing harms on non-responsible members of criminal groups than the self-defence analogy would first suggest.[5]

In any case, in reality, there will be limits to the analogy of non-responsible threats in organised crime. On both the agency and unjust threat views, it still makes a difference whether a person is a part of a threat, even non-culpably, or is merely an innocent bystander. One can expect that, for our purposes, the category of people who are both (a) a part of a criminal threat, but (b) not at all responsible for it, is relatively small. Those who are not responsible will tend to be classed as innocent bystanders. According to one prominent account of group responsibility, it is a necessary condition of being a member of a responsibility-bearing group that one has knowledge of the wrongdoing of the group.[6] If so, then the unknowing innocent at the periphery of the group should not be classed as a part of the threat at all. This is a meaningful result. Insofar as police impose significant setbacks upon people who are innocent of any threat, they will struggle to argue that there is liability at work. This has a significant bearing on any proportionality assessment. It means that such harms will be especially difficult to justify.

2 Proportionality and the minimally responsible

Some of the most controversial cases of undercover policing involve imposition of serious, life-changing setbacks upon those who are minimally responsible for a threat. Intuitively, proportionality in self-defence involves comparing not only the harm threatened and the harm used to avert the threat but also the attacker's culpability for the threat. One whose slight negligence gives rise to a threat of some small harm, H, makes himself liable to less defensive harm than one who maliciously aims at H. On this view, just as a higher degree of culpability makes a threat liable to a greater self-defensive force, so also does a higher degree of culpability make a criminal liable to more intrusive or harmful investigative practices. On this understanding of proportionate undercover policing, one does not forfeit all of one's rights against being harmed simply in virtue of being any threat at all. One becomes more liable to intrusion and

manipulation where, other things being equal, one is more responsible for the possible harm that is to be prevented.[7]

However, there is a different way of looking at this issue. It may be
that once a person has some responsibility for some wrong, even if it
is a relatively small part of the responsibility, then she becomes liable
to intrusive policing responses to the degree that such responses are
effective in preventing the wrong. On this view, responsibility functions like a gate: once one has gone through the gate and entered into
criminal enterprise, one loses one's complaint against police-imposed
setbacks, so long as those setbacks are efficient means to legitimate
policing ends. Since it can be efficacious for undercover policing to
target those at the fringes of criminal groups, this view entails that those
at the fringes who are minimally responsible for the wrong at hand can
be liable to a great deal of the harms of undercover policing.

In the context of personal self-defence and war, Jeff McMahan
has defended a version of the principles underlying this view. The
idea is that when one member of a group must come to harm, and
the harm cannot be divided among the parties, then the person who
is the *most* responsible for fact that a harm must occur is liable to
suffer it. If responsibility lies anywhere, it is with the party who
has made it the case that a harm may occur, however, blamelessly.[8]
As McMahan puts it: 'Even if one bears some responsibility for an
unavoidable harm that cannot be divided, one may not be liable to
suffer the harm if someone else is more responsible.'[9] In the context
of war, this means that combatants can be liable to be killed where
non-combatants are not, even though non-combatants can bear some
responsibility for the creation of an unjust threat if they vote for mili-
tary action. In the context of undercover policing, it might be argued
that this idea implies that those with minimal responsibility at the
periphery of a criminal group can be liable to a great deal of intrusion
if this is necessary to prevent the crime involved, since those at the
periphery of the criminal group are more responsible than the victims
of the crime that it perpetuates. Suppose that police have few leads
in addressing an active terrorist group. They can *either* (a) deploy an
undercover agent to befriend and take advantage of a person who is
not only known to have social links to the group, and who has spoken
positively about them, but is also vulnerable and unlikely to become
actively involved, *or* (b) do nothing. On the relative responsibility
view, the person in (a) is liable to the relevant harm.

However, there are three reasons to doubt the conclusion that the minimally responsible are liable to such significant harms in the context of undercover policing. First, the choice is unlikely to be as clear-cut as described in the example earlier. As I argued in the previous chapter, the applicability of the necessity condition is unclear in conditions of uncertainty, and police are always in conditions of uncertainty. It may be the case that police can act in a way that has a slightly lower chance of success, but that involves significantly less direct harm to the target. If so, it is difficult to parse the idea that only the former approach is necessary to avert the threat.

Second, we may read these cases as ones in which those at the centre of the target criminal group are the most responsible for the threats. The example supposes that targeting these individuals directly is not possible. As soon as this changes in the course of the operation, then the moral balance will change too. As the infiltration develops, the justification for imposing harm on those at the periphery will quickly evaporate.

Third, there are reasons to doubt the relative responsibility idea in general. It seems to have the implication that there is no limit on the number of minimally responsible individuals who can be liable to be harmed. Suppose that instead of just targeting one individual at the periphery of a criminal group, the best hope for an investigation is for undercover officers to target hundreds or more people who are minimally responsible. For example, organised crime groups can aggressively recruit users as dealers, thereby avoiding the need to interact directly with customers. Those exploited in this way may be controlled with the threat of an over-concentrated dose, and thereby serious harm or death, should they be suspected of revealing any information about the members of the central group.[10] Suppose that undercover police begin their infiltration by targeting many of these individuals, seeking, in the first place, ways to find trust and manipulate them into revealing information about the central criminal group. Now, *if* people in this type of situation are minimally responsible for the work of the broader group (which will depend on the particular circumstances and especially on the degree of coercion that they have suffered), and if the ongoing harms of the central criminal group are sufficiently heinous,[11] then we *might* accept, on the relative responsibility view, that such people are liable to this kind of manipulation. But suppose that the best way to infiltrate the group is to target *all* of the user-dealers. The relative responsibility view seems to allow this, as, again, all are liable. But this seems disproportionate.[12]

In this and the previous section, I have discussed the proportionality of intruding upon those at the fringes of criminal groups. I have distinguished between the non-responsible and the minimally responsible. Quite different principles are at work in those two cases. In the former case, there is a possible argument that the innocent is a part of a threat. In the latter case, there is an argument that the burdens of addressing a threat should fall upon the most responsible possible cost-bearer. However, in both cases, I have argued that it is difficult to draw out these arguments in such a way that they have the practical implication that people at the peripheries are liable to undercover policing.

3   Consequentially justified harms

In the remainder of this chapter, I discuss the idea that justified undercover policing involves committing wrongs. According to the liability view, it is possible for justified undercover policing to involve the imposition of setbacks upon those who are not liable to them. This goes beyond the possibilities canvassed in the previous two sections, where I considered the possibility that innocent third parties or innocent associates of those involved in serious crime may be liable to the setbacks of undercover policing. Here, I consider the possibility that people can have setbacks justifiably imposed upon them to which they are not liable, including those that are greater than those to which they have made themselves liable. As we have seen, it is often advantageous in constructing an undercover operation to focus initial efforts upon the 'weak links' of an organisation: those at its periphery who have minor involvement in and commitment to it but who may nonetheless provide channels of access to its core.

Consequentially justified harms are those that are imposed upon people who are not liable (or greater harms than the harms to which they are liable), where the harms are justified by a preponderance of good consequences. Even where there are no grounds for suspicion of involvement in wrongdoing, or even positive evidence of innocence, it is still possible that the harms of undercover policing are useful and justified. This justification will need to cross the high bar of the kind that is analogous to a justification of harming an innocent bystander for the sake of some very significant benefit. Consider a seriously harmful criminal organisation that is highly forensically aware and has shown that it has effective counter-surveillance measures. An opportunity arises to infiltrate the group that involves befriending a minimally responsible delivery driver and manipulating him into a relationship of trust. Suppose that the driver is unlikely to be successfully recruited as an informant.[13] The wrong of manipulation can then be overwhelmed by the good of disrupting the criminal organisation.

There are two ways that we can understand the overwhelming of a *pro tanto* wrong. First, there is a *balancing* model. According to this conception, in the larger scheme of things, the value of the wrong of the police action is far less than the value of the good that it brings about, and, as the action is thereby justified, there is no residual wrong. Analogously, an investment that carries a small fee, but produces a large dividend, provides, on balance, monetary value. There is nothing to regret about the fee, except for the possibility that more profit might have been made elsewhere.[14] Second, and alternatively, there is a *lesser evil* model. This is different. In such cases, a residual wrong remains, even if the police action was, all things considered, justified. The lesser of two evils remains an evil, and an appropriate object of regret. In this spirit, Joseph Raz argues that conflicts of values can have the 'unfortunate' implication that it is impossible to comply with all of the reasons one faces.[15] In such cases, one should 'come as close to complete conformity [with reason] as possible', but it remains the case that one can rationally regret one's action, and that those harmed by it can have claims to compensation. A complaint can remain in such cases. A person's right is infringed upon, and the justification is a broader benefit.

If undercover harms can sometimes be justified by their overwhelming good consequences, we can expect that the balancing model is often at work. This is especially the case where the harms are small or moderate. Nonetheless, I suggest that the phenomenology of grievances of the non-responsible and minimally responsible subjects of seriously intrusive undercover police work that is justified by overwhelming good consequences are well captured by the second model of justified *pro tanto* wrongs, that of the lesser evil justification. If this is right, then the view I am putting forward allows that police can justifiably act in ways that, in one way, wrong people. To be sure, not all of the setbacks of undercover police are like this. First, many will be imposed upon people who are liable to such treatment. Second, I have suggested that small wrongs can be legitimised through consent, and so we need not say that these involve a wrong. And third, even those harms justified merely by consequences may be justified on the balancing model. Nonetheless, the lesser evil category remains. Before we examine the implications of this, consider a further way in which the phenomenon arises.

4 Epistemically justified wrongs

Alongside consequentially justified harms, there is another kind of possible justified police wrong. The structure of the view that I have set out involves an appeal to liability. Liability is not, however, transparent. Indeed, a function of undercover police work is to *identify* liability, or, at least, to uncover the facts that would enable one to make an informed judgment of liability. There is a so-called ladder of intelligence, whereby some information leads to a greater understanding of where resources should be deployed so as best to gain more relevant information, and so forth. Since moral liability to intrusion often cannot be known before an operation is authorised or an officer acts, undercover work will involve taking moral risks, whereby intrusions and manipulations will be visited upon individuals whose liability can only be known after the fact.

We can justifiably impose some risks on each other. Consider the act of driving. By choosing to stay at home, or to walk or cycle instead, I would impose little or no risk at all. By choosing to drive, I impose a very small risk on pedestrians and other drivers. In these cases, we lack knowledge of whether the risk will actualise. If it does, is a *pro tanto* wrong committed? Seemingly not in the driving case. I argued earlier (in Chapter 3) that police actions should be judged according to what evidence they reasonably ought to have possessed. Epistemically justified wrongs involve an action that, *ex ante*, is permissible, having taken reasonable steps to obtain knowledge about the action's effects, but, *ex post*, is impermissible.[16]

Epistemically justified wrongs are especially likely to arise when it is only possible to prevent a significant harm by acting on incomplete information. Imagine a group of five people have grounds for believing, with 90% credibility, that they are under a serious threat, and that they can only prevent harm to themselves by imposing a serious harm on their perceived attacker. If it turns out that the threat was a mirage, and also that the purported attacker is not responsible for the warranted belief that there is a likely threat, then we tend to say that a wrong is imposed upon her if defensive harm is used. In this case, the defensive actions of the five are epistemically justified, but the person that they harm retains a complaint against them; she undergoes a *pro tanto* wrong.

It may be that there are cases where the probability of acting rightly is sufficiently high that one does not commit a wrong where the outcome harms another. As we have seen, right action is not purely fact relative. However, police are often in circumstances in which there is a high degree of uncertainty. The imperative to act to prevent a harm warrants the moral risk, but it is also clear that there *is* a moral risk.[17]

5   Wrongs and reparations

In the cases of both epistemically justified wrongs and consequentially justified harms, a moral complaint remains about policing actions that are justified. If there is a complaint, then one would expect that there is a claim for reparation. In this section, I explore what form this may take and consider arguments against reparation.

Recall, in Chapter 2, I canvassed the idea that undercover policing involves a tragic clash of values. This is an idea that appears from within the ranks of both undercover police and also its critics: the practice of seriously manipulating people involves wrongs that cannot be weighed against the benefits that they provide. I argued that this view is unsatisfying in part because it does seem that we can say more about how the values interact. An interesting view on entrapment and dirty hands is put forward by Tanyi et al. drawing on the work of Kis.[18] According to this position, it is possible for there to be acts that are not only seriously wrongful but also morally required, and the right way to consider these is not in terms of how we should act, but in terms of the appropriate reactions: 'The act is morally reprehensible but the proper response to this is not blame but regret or remorse. And the outsider's ("our") proper response are not resentment and indignation but fear and pity.'[19] Nonetheless, alongside an analysis of appropriate reactive attitudes, the matter of reparations also arises. If there is a *pro tanto* wrong, it is difficult to see why there would not be a corresponding obligation of reparation. In discussions of war and self-defence, this issue has received relatively little attention, likely because the harms involved in war are so serious that compensation is typically impossible.[20]

In general, one would expect that an appropriate form of recompense would be available to those who have a legitimate complaint. Putting a similar idea in different language, Jennifer Page argues that there can be a gap between the legality and morality of police actions, and that even where police act within the law, a moral wrong can remain: 'even if an officer acted reasonably, the non-liability of the person killed itself has moral significance. By definition, a non-liable person does not "deserve" to be killed.'[21] What are appropriate forms of recompense for the kinds of harms involved in undercover policing? I will consider monetary compensation later. Consider first that the harms are usually, at base, *social*, and one would accordingly expect reparation to include social means. That is, the harms involve undermining a person's sense of their self and their ability to form trustworthy relationships. The goal of reparation is to repair: to bring matters closer to the situation that existed before the wrong was committed, while accepting that a wrong *was* committed, and that the situation that previously existed may be unobtainable.

There are three means by which this kind of repair may take place. The first is the provision of *information*. Those subject to manipulation by undercover police report a sense of disorientation. By having access to specific details of how they were treated, the manipulated may begin to rebuild their capacity to make judgments of the social world around them; where details are withheld, they will lack a tool with which to overcome or mitigate an ongoing sense that those they meet are untrustworthy. Second, alongside information, it can be valuable to have *recognition* that one was subject to a *pro tanto* wrong. To be a lone voice asserting victimhood is quite different to being publicly recognised as having undergone a harm that, even if it was justified by its expected good consequences elsewhere, was a harm to which one was not liable. This kind of reparation facilitates the rebuilding of the ability to form trusting relationships by diminishing the need for the manipulated to explain themselves and to argue for their corner. An absence of recognition of a wrong leaves responsibility for identifying and explaining the moral residue in the hands of the victim.

Third, the ritual of *apology* has reparative properties.[22] Stronger than recognition, apology involves an express statement of culpability and an expression of regret, and has a function of facilitating healing of relations between the wrongdoer and the wronged. In the case under consideration, apology may aid in rebuilding the relationship between the state and the citizen who has undergone a *pro tanto* wrong. It may be asked how there can be a meaningful apology where police have acted justifiably, all things considered. I suggest that we can make sense of this idea drawing on personal cases with precisely the structure that we are considering. If one hurts someone innocent in pursuit of a goal that is justified by its general good consequences, it is not abnormal to repair relations with apology. It may be clumsy but correct to say 'I'm sorry. I had to do that because it saved someone's life', and it may be normal to feel guilt about one's treatment of the person that one has harmed in so acting.[23]

The compensation idea tells against the *exceptionless* policy of 'neither confirm nor deny' (NCND) that is claimed by police in the UK in this regard.[24] The policy has been a key battleground in debates between police and claimants in the ongoing Undercover Policing Inquiry. The NCND policy precludes the first step towards recognition of these wrongs that are a part of police activity.[25] To be sure, there will be cases in which security considerations will override the reason for transparency about the facts of an expired investigation. However, our current context is one in which there is precedent for the release of more information in a way that does not threaten security.[26] The next step would be a positive institutional effort at identification of information that can be released to those who have been wronged in this way. The point is that there are cases in which police owe people information if they can possibly provide it; that in any weighing of values, it should be accepted that this information can be highly valuable to people; and that there are some subtle possible policies that are compatible with security concerns than blanket refusals to provide information. This is especially the case where we allow the passage of time. Once twenty or thirty years have passed, and the officers involved are distanced from undercover work, and the relevant operations are no longer in process, one would increasingly expect ways to reveal information without putting officers at risk.

Should reparation go beyond recognition, information, and apology? In other contexts in which the state imposes without sufficient justification the kinds of harmful wrongs that I have set out in Chapters 1 and 2, people can demand monetary compensation. Why are police not liable for such compensation when they get things wrong? It is difficult to see why not, in principle. Although it may be the case that psychological harm is qualitatively different to monetary compensation, we are quite used in other areas – not least, in tort law – to finding ways to make one commensurate with the other. It might be responded that a practice of compensation would incentivise people to associate with organised criminals in a non-culpable way, thereby giving a public policy reason against its use. However, this is a speculative suggestion and there may be specific policy responses available to mitigate it.

The strongest reason against monetary compensation is the following. It may be that a lesser evil justification only works where compensation is not paid. That is, it may be the case that the practice of undercover policing often has highly beneficial good consequences, but these consequences would be severely diminished or eliminated were full compensation paid to non-liable individuals who are harmed in the course of such policing. Among the lesser evils of some undercover policing, on this account, is the wrong of not making amends for one's wrongs. This structure involves the wrong of failing to make amends being less than the cost of making amends.

To be sure, this does not rule out monetary compensation across the board. I am working within a framework aimed at understanding how an ideal police force can carry out undercover work legitimately, and have identified activities that, *even though they are justified all things considered*, warrant reparation. Where police have acted in ways that are not, in the final analysis, justified – involving brutality or abuse, for example – a lesser evil justification for non-compensation is overwhelmed by the importance of making amends.

It may be objected to my position as follows. I have said that the police may carry out lesser evil wrongs, where the balance is especially stark, that they carry out *pro tanto* wrongs in doing so, that they owe reparation for these wrongs, that complete compensation may often be impossible,[27] but that police, nonetheless, may carry out these wrongs, as they are justified all things considered. Some will reply that police ought not to carry out these wrongs because police should not do wrong. And similarly, the possibility of epistemically justified wrongs shows that police should not be in the business that they are in, since policing carried out even with reasonable care involves predictably committing wrongs.

This argument could be taken in one of two ways. It may be that lesser evil justifications are *never* good justifications. Rights infringements are never justified, regardless of what is at stake. However, in other areas, we do not take this view. Only extremists argue that rights trump consequences, whatever the consequences. As Rawls says, any ethical system that fails to take account of the value of consequences is 'irrational'.[28] Alternatively, the argument could be that lesser evil justifications are possible when and only when full or near-full compensation is possible. This view rules out lesser evil justifications that involve death or very serious harm, where recompense is impossible, and so dramatically reduces their scope, bringing it closer to the more extreme view. Moreover, the view is difficult to motivate, once we consider the question of *who* should compensate. By harming some in order to prevent greater harm to others, on this view, one creates an obligation that the person who is harmed is compensated. Whoever now has the obligation to compensate – whether it is the beneficiaries, oneself in causing the harm, or some aggregate of the community – there is now an unfairness of a setback on the part of those doing the compensating. It is unclear why the compensating 'evil' is justified but not the evil of being harmed.

The view that I have set out, then, incorporates a dirty hands element. There *is* a moral residue in undercover policing. By appealing to the idea of liability, I have reduced but not eliminated it. Many are liable to the treatment they receive, but not all, and reparation can be due but can also be justifiably incomplete or absent. *To this extent*, the sense expressed by some undercover officers that they are performing wrongs in the service of a broader value is an accurate reflection of the ethical situation.

6   Accepting police wrongs

I have argued that police can justifiably infringe on people's rights in the course of their work. There is a pair of problems for the idea that police commit *pro tanto* wrongs in the normal course of their duties: the problem of resistance and the problem of democracy.

The issue of resistance is separate from the issue of compensation. One can be due compensation for the harm associated with some action, while also being under an obligation not to resist it. The problem is that if there are 'lesser evil' wrongs in the normal run of undercover policing, then the legitimacy of the institution of undercover policing is seriously damaged. It is plausible that it is a general principle that one has a right to defend oneself if one is being wrongfully threatened with harm. If the police are wrongfully causing harm (in the form of impositions that are imperfectly justified by the preponderance of good consequences elsewhere, or through beliefs that are epistemically warranted for the purposes of an investigation, but false), then it seems that those who are subject to the harms have a right to self-defence against police.[29]

On the face of things, this provides a challenge to undercover policing. Those who realise that they are wrongfully the subject of deception and manipulation thereby have a right to resist the police – but isn't part of the function of the police to have a monopoly on coercion?[30] We can understand the idea that one may resist police who are acting in ways that display, for example, racist violence. But can we make sense of a situation in which people have a right to resist police who are acting in accordance with the best principles? Something has to give: either the existence of the police as we normally conceive of them, or the right to resist wrongs.

One possible response to the problem of resistance holds that there are exceptions to the principle that one has a right to defend against responsible threats when one has agreed to allow a higher authority to adjudicate. Thus, rather than using force oneself, one should call the police. However, in the present case, that response is unsuccessful. It is the police themselves who are the agents of the wrong.

Another possible response to the problem urges that the types of resistance that are proportionate are not violent. One is permitted to respond proportionately by tricking the officer, feigning compliance, and so forth. This is not an obviously implausible outcome.

It may cover a large part of the cases of justifiable resistance to rights infringements by undercover police that are justified by their overwhelming good consequences. It seems coercion is not proportionate as a response to the typical harms associated with undercover policing. This response thereby mitigates the problem. However, some of the harms of undercover police are strong. If these are justified in lesser evil terms, then the proportionate response will also be strong. It may be in principle problematic that people can justifiably impose strong harms on police in response to justified police actions.

Furthermore, it may be argued that self-defence that actively causes new harms is harder to justify than self-defence that eliminates existing threats.[31] Accordingly, justified but non-liable targets can resist in ways that undermine a police operation, but it is harder for them to justify resistance that actively causes new harms. In practice, as I argue in Chapter 6, it is difficult to set up plausible cases in which police justifiably impose serious setbacks upon the non-liable. This problem is therefore smaller than it first appears.

Alongside the problem of resistance, there is a second problem following from the idea that police carry out justified wrongs, the problem of *democracy*. The view I am proposing incorporates a type of dirty hands position. There are wrongs in the functioning of police work. These may be compensable but not always or entirely. Whatever an ideal police force looks like, one can suppose that it would exist through the consent of those who are being policed. Classically, the first fully instituted police force, London's Metropolitan Police, was formally guided by the Peelian principle that police act as servants of citizens; in the United States, the police force carries that slogan 'Protect and Serve'. The force of such ideas is to put policing within the remit of democracy.[32]

Now, there is some range of rules that can be democratically agreed to, and some rules that cannot be agreed to as democratic, even where they gain the assent of a majority. It is widely considered undemocratic for a minority to be exploited by a majority. The challenge that arises is this. If undercover police operate according to a set of rules that are democratically approved, how can they commit *pro tanto* wrongs in doing so? Consequentially justified harms and epistemically justified wrongs could be faced by any citizen, and (by hypothesis) are imposed by police as part of a legitimately democratic system that is beneficial to all. Why, then, are those who

are harmed or have their interests set back by the undercover policing structure *wronged* where all act justifiably? On the other hand, if
an undercover policing structure is democratically approved by the
citizenry but involves committing wrongs at its core, isn't it more
like the case of the tyrannous majority, a principle that carries a
semblance of democracy in its majoritarianism, but fails to meet the
standards of democracy because it improperly imposes great costs
on a few?

Consider first how this problem applies in the case of epistemically justified wrongs. The tyrannous majority acts deliberately. The
undercover police are imposing open risks in the case of epistemically justified wrongs. Statistically, it is a near certainty that some
will be wronged where they are not liable to be harmed. But such
statistical chances of harm are commonly judged to be easier to justify than impositions of known harms, or indeed of closed risks of
harm, in which it is certain some individual (or individuals) will be
harmed, but it is not known whom. Indeed, it is taken as a data point
in discussion on the ethics of risk imposition that there is such a difference between open and closed risks, with the challenge being to
explain it.[33]

In the case of consequentially justified harms, it is not possible to take only the perspective of the imposition of a known risk.
Police are imposing risks from a certain viewpoint – the institution of undercover policing as a whole imposes this risk – but in
individual cases there may be an absolute certainty about the situation. *This* specific named person is going to be manipulated so that
greater intelligence can be gained about crimes for which she is
not culpable. In such a case, she is wronged, *pro tanto*, and is due
a form of compensation – and the challenge remains: if the system
at its heart involves wronging some individuals, then it cannot be
properly democratically assented to; if it does not involve wronging
some individuals, then they have no claim for compensation.

However, this argument has a strong central premise that is difficult to ground. The central premise is that it is not possible for there
to be democratic assent to institutions that use lesser evil justifications for their actions. If an act is justified all things considered, then
it is difficult to see why it cannot be a subject of legitimate democratic assent. Supposing that there is a real category of justified rights
infringements, we need a further reason why such actions are ruled

out of public action. If our moral universe does contain elements of dirty hands, then this applies to the decisions that politicians must make, and accordingly, to the decisions about what kind of politics to endorse on the part of the voting population. Accordingly, the result is not that democratic dirty hands are impossible, but that the taint – and resulting obligations to recompense where possible – apply to citizens as well as to those within power.[34] If this is right, then the problem of dirty hands is one that citizens and rules share, and in the ideal police force, the responsibility for justified police wrongs is taken on by the citizenry as a whole.

7   Concluding note

In this chapter, I have examined the implications of the liability view in two areas: its application to those at the periphery of criminal groups, and the way that it might imply an obligation of reparation on the part of the police. In the next chapter, I examine more closely the ethics of the manipulative element of undercover policing.

Notes

1 Consider also the broad intelligence gathering exercises involved in infiltrations: O'Neill, Megan, and Bethan Loftus. 'Policing and the Surveillance of the Marginal: Everyday Contexts of Social Control'. *Theoretical Criminology* 17, no. 4 (1 November 2013): 437–54.

2 E.g., McMahan, Jeff. 'The Basis of Moral Liability to Defensive Killing'. *Philosophical Issues* 15, no. 1 (2005): 386–405.

3 E.g., Thomson, Judith Jarvis. 'Self-Defense'. *Philosophy & Public Affairs* (1991): 283–310.

4 Quong, J. 'Agent-Relative Prerogatives to Do Harm'. *Criminal Law and Philosophy* 10, no. 4 (2016): 815–29.

5 To be sure, many in the literature on self-defence avoid appeal to agent-centred prerogatives in this way, accepting that one acts wrongly in defending one's life where the only way to do so is to kill an innocent threat.

6 List, Christian, and Philip Pettit. *Group Agency: The Possibility, Design, and Status of Corporate Agents*. Oxford: Oxford University Press, 2011.

7 For somewhat different position, see Quong, Jonathan. 'Proportionality, Liability, and Defensive Harm'. *Philosophy & Public Affairs* 43, no. 2 (1 March 2015): 144–73. On Quong's view, the mode of agency, and not responsibility, is a factor in determining a proportionate self-defensive response.

8 Mcmahan, Jeff. Killing in War. Oxford: Oxford University Press, 2009. For discussion and criticisms of this idea see Lazar, Seth. 'Responsibility, Risk, and Killing in Self-Defense'. Ethics 119, no. 4 (2009): 699–728.

9 Mcmahan, J. 'Who Is Morally Liable to Be Killed in War'. Analysis 71, no. 3 (1 July 2011): 544–59, p. 552.

10 According to a prominent memoir of an undercover officer, this situation is not uncommon, and existed in Brighton in the 2000s. Woods, Neil, and J. S. Rafaeli. Good Cop, Bad War. London: Random House, 2016.

11 Drug prohibition is, as noted in ch.1, questionable, partly because of the incentives that it creates for criminal groups – I suspend this point for the sake of the example here.

12 This argument tracks Bazargan, Saba. 'Killing Minimally Responsible Threats'. Ethics 125, no. 1 (October 2014): 114–36.

13 The recruitment may be unsuccessful because the driver is seen as recalcitrant – a factor that could increase his responsibility. Or, it may be that the driver rationally fears the risks involved in informing – a factor that diminishes his responsibility and also may increase the wrong of manipulation, as it imposes a risk on the subject. A successful cashing out of this example would need to balance these factors.

14 Reisner points out that the best understanding of the etymology of the *pro tanto* obligation involves it being possible for it to be fully outweighed within some domain. Reisner, A. E. Prima Facie and Pro Tanto Oughts. International Encyclopedia of Ethics. Oxford: Blackwell, 2013.

15 Raz, J. 'Personal Practical Conflicts'. In Practical Conflicts: New Philosophical Essays, edited by P. Baumann and M. Betzler. Cambridge: Cambridge University Press, 2004.

16 See Mcmahan, Jeff. 'Self-Defense and Culpability'. Law and Philosophy 24, 6 (2005): 751–74, p. 771; see also Ferzan, Kimberly Kessler. 'Justifying Self-Defense'. Law and Philosophy 24, no. 6 (2005): 711–49, p. 728.

17 Compare the view in Miller, Seumas, and Ian A. Gordon. Investigative Ethics: Ethics for Police Detectives and Criminal Investigators. Oxford: Wiley-Blackwell, 2014. It is argued as follows: 'sometimes persons reasonably suspected of committing crimes are in fact innocent. However, innocent persons wrongly suspected of crimes are not harmed by the police in the knowledge that they are innocent. So we do not have intentional harming of persons known to be innocent. Rather, we have intentional harming of persons thought likely to be guilty; and we have unintended harming of the innocent as a by-product of police work. Troublesome as this is, it does not put immorality at the core of the police function' (p. 266). On my view, there is space for a case in which a person who is wrongly but reasonably suspected retains a complaint.

18 Tanyi, Attila, Stephen K. McLeod, and Daniel J. Hill. 'The Ethics of Entrapment: A Dirty Hands Problem?'. Unpublished MS. https://philpapers.org/archive/TANTEO-16.pdf (accessed May 2021); Kis, J. Politics as a Moral Problem. Budapest, Hungary: CEU Press, 2008.

19 Ibid., p. 19.
20 McMahan, Jeff. and Saba Bazargan both expressly take the view that compensation is owed where people are harmed with lesser evil justifications. 'Self-Defense against Justified Threateners'. In How We Fight, edited by Helen Frowe and Gerald Lang, Oxford: Oxford University Press, 2014, pp. 104–37; Bazargan, Saba. 'Killing Minimally Responsible Threats'. Ethics 125, no. 1 (October 2014): 114–36.
21 Page, Jennifer M. 'Reparations for Police Killings'. Perspectives on Politics 17, no. 4 (2019): 7.
22 For a treatment of this idea see Bennett, Christopher. The Apology Ritual: A Philosophical Theory of Punishment, Cambridge: Cambridge University Press, 2008.
23 If one takes the view that when *pro tanto* wrongs are outweighed, they are always outweighed by comparable considerations, then this apology will not be coherent and guilt will not be apposite. Whether one sees apologies as meaningful in these cases is an indicator of whether one accepts the characterisation of 'lesser evils' that I have offered.
24 College of Policing. 'Undercover Policing Authorised Professional Practice', February 2021, §6.5.1. https://library.college.police.uk/docs/college-of-policing/APP-Undercover-policing-February-2021.pdf (accessed May 2021). For a developed argument against the policy see Hadjimatheou, Katerina. 'Neither Confirm Nor Deny: Secrecy and Disclosure in Undercover Policing'. Criminal Justice Ethics 36, no. 3 (2017): 279–96.
25 Formally, the justification for withholding information from interested parties should occur on a case-by-case basis, and not with reference to a blanket policy of 'neither confirm nor deny'. McKay, Simon. Covert Policing: Law and Practice. 2nd edition. Oxford: Oxford University Press, 2015, pp. 379–80.
26 See the large effort to this end within the Undercover Policing Inquiry.
27 Complete compensation may be conceived of in different ways. Does it involve being indifferent between the *ex post* and *ex ante* position? Or does it involve having the same actual goods? The latter will often be impossible in the case of undercover policing harms. And if it is difficult to make sense of compensation for wrongly moving a person along an indifference curve, then full compensation will often be unavailable. See Goodin, R. 'Theories of Compensation'. Oxford Journal of Legal Studies 9 (1989): 56–75.
28 Rawls, John. A Theory of Justice. Revised edition. Cambridge, MA: Harvard University Press, 1999, p. 26.
29 For a defence of the latter view, see Brennan, J. When All Else Fails: The Ethics of Resistance to State Injustice. Princeton, NJ: Princeton University Press, 2018.
30 These are, of course, cases in which undercover policing has failed, since the officer's identity is revealed.
31 In the context of self-defence in the trolley problem, compare: Jeff, McMahan. 'Self-Defence against Justified Threateners'. In How We

Fight: Ethics in War, edited by Helen Frowe and Gerald Lang. Oxford: Oxford University Press, 2014; Frowe, Helen. 'Lesser-Evil Justifications for Harming: Why We're Required to Turn the Trolley'. The Philosophical Quarterly 68, no. 272 (2018); Steinhoff, Uwe. 'The Liability of Justified Attackers'. Ethical Theory and Moral Practice 19, no. 4 (August 2016): 1015–30.

32 For an account of these principles and a call to harness them for meaningful regulative action, see Loader, Ian. 'In Search of Civic Policing: Recasting the "Peelian" Principles'. Criminal Law and Philosophy 10, no. 3 (1 September 2016): 427–40.

33 Lenman, James. 'Contractualism and Risk Imposition'. Politics, Philosophy & Economics 7, no. 1 (2008): 99–122; Tadros, Victor. 'Controlling Risk'. In Prevention and the Limits of the Criminal Law, edited by Andrew Ashworth, Lucia Zedner, and Patrick Tomlin. Oxford: Oxford University Press, 2013, pp. 133–55.

34 Wijze, Stephen de. 'The Problem of Democratic Dirty Hands: Citizen Complicity, Responsibility, and Guilt'. The Monist 101, no. 2 (1 April 2018): 129–49; Archard, David. 'Dirty Hands and the Complicity of the Democratic Public'. Ethical Theory and Moral Practice 16, no. 4 (1 August 2013): 777–90.

5   Manipulation

1   Introduction

In his memoir of his time as an undercover officer, Joe Carter describes an operation that was aimed as infiltrating criminal groups. He developed a partnership with a man, Ray, who was dealing large quantities of drugs. Ray indicated that he had connections in dealing in weapons. Carter contrived to be arrested on suspicion of money laundering for carrying £50,000 in cash. Once released, he confronted Ray angrily, telling him that there must be an informant, and that it must be either Ray or the contact he was due to meet. As predicted, after forcefully denying that he was a snitch, Ray suggested that the contact needed to be 'got', and that he could help Carter by putting him in touch with someone who would supply a weapon with a silencer. This way, Carter deepened his infiltration and gained credible access to a more serious layer of criminality.[1]

Carter could have simply concocted a story and asked to purchase a weapon. However, through the subterfuge of being arrested and then putting Ray in the position of denying that he had broken trust, Carter added a layer of believability to his role and put psychological pressure upon Ray. He thereby made the tentative business of buying an illegal firearm much more likely to succeed. Carter created a situation in which he knew that Ray was likely to suggest, even if casually, the need for violence. Demonstrating preparedness to facilitate such an act is a way for him to remove the supposed suspicion that Carter has of him. Carter successfully exploited this criminal norm.

One thing that can make undercover policing so outrageous when it is carried out illegitimately is its manipulative element. In their

DOI: 10.4324/9780429293443-5

infiltrative and proactive sting roles, undercover officers seek to obtain actions from their targets, to lead people to behave in ways that are consonant with policing goals. In our day to day lives, using trickery and pressure in order to obtain actions from people that aim at some other end – even if there is an on-balance benefit – is the wrong kind of way to relate to people; it is a *prima facie* wrong. Imagine a charity fundraiser who deliberately targets people who seem vulnerable, who dissembles or lies about the charitable cause in accordance with what it seems people want to hear, who exploits social norms of politeness in the extreme, and who creates a false sense of urgency about the need to donate. Even if it is better if people's money is in the hands of the charity, the fundraiser commits wrongs in the way it is solicited. If there are limits on manipulativeness elsewhere, beyond mere cost-benefit considerations, what are the limits on police manipulativeness?

As well as the case of Ray, recall the cases described in Chapter 1, in which police deliberately form intimate bonds with their targets, going so far as to have children with them.[2] The ostensible goal of these operations was, as with the case of Ray, infiltrative: the proffered justification is that it provides access to *other* people who are involved in more serious crimes.

There is an understandable tendency in discussions of police manipulation to focus on entrapment, that is, on prosecution and punishment for acts that police have encouraged. Nonetheless, in this chapter I argue that we should broaden the perspective. Entrapment is not all that is wrong with police manipulation, and indeed it is not clear that entrapment is always wrong itself. My view is both stronger and more permissive than the mainstream. My view can permit what may be regarded as entrapment when there is liability. But it opposes manipulation in certain cases even when the effects are benign and emphasises the importance of restricting manipulations even when prosecution is not a goal.

2 Beyond entrapment

Manipulative police actions can aim to prevent or disrupt criminal activity without immediately expecting or obtaining an arrest.[3] This can occur where it is expected that there will be insufficient evidence for a prosecution, or where obtaining such evidence would be risky or resource-intensive. Police actions can aim at gaining information, or access to information, about other individuals. Suppose an undercover agent engineers a friendship with a person on the periphery of a criminal group with the goal of establishing credibility with those who are more central to that group. The manipulated person might not even be on the periphery of the criminal group, but rather, the criminal group may be on the periphery of the group of the person who is being manipulated. An undercover officer might accept religious instruction with the goal of establishing his credentials for the purposes of obtaining a governing position within a group whose small extremist wing he eventually aims to infiltrate.[4]

The etymology of 'entrapment' encourages the understanding that it means: (a) the manipulation into criminal behaviour, (b) for which the arrest and prosecution of the target is sought. That is, a person is *trapped* by police. A mechanism is set up, and the otherwise innocent person walks into it. However, the concept is occasionally used without element (b). Entrapment, on this understanding, simply is the manipulation into a criminal (or perhaps merely wrongful) act, even where there is no aspiration to arrest the target for that act. The distinction is significant because legitimate policing purposes, including those that can be manifested with manipulative strategies, often do not aim directly at an arrest of the target. Instead, they can seek to disrupt, prevent, or facilitate the gathering of intelligence, and in doing so might, in principle, wrongfully manipulate.

The concept of 'agent provocateur' is broader than the concept of entrapment. It refers to police manipulation of people into behaviour that is against their interests or purposes.[5] Agent provocateur activity can also include the encouragement of groups into behaviour that will damage their reputation. For example, undercover police may infiltrate a group and spread rumours so as to divide and disrupt the group, or even to turn public opinion against them. Similarly, a group's purposes can be subverted where an agent provocateur gains a position of influence within a group and encourages counterproductive activity. Entrapment, as defined here, then, is a form of agent provocateur activity. The latter involves police manipulation into activity that is against the target's interests or purposes; the former involves police manipulation into arrest. Police activity extends beyond direct efforts to achieve arrests, and people's interests can be set back without arresting them.

The existence of police purpose beyond immediate prosecution gives reason to examine manipulation in general. The issues raised by the practice by police of forming of intimate bonds with protesters are not adequately covered by discussion of entrapment. Even without any effort on the part of police to guide people into committing criminal acts, a serious harm is caused by these practices. Similarly, in the case of Ray described earlier, circumstances are created in which the target encourages and facilitates violence. Even if the goal is not to create a prosecution of Ray, there remains a question about the legitimacy of going to significant lengths to create the social and psychological conditions in which it is expected that a citizen will propose serious harm or murder.

The literature on entrapment proper, where there is a goal of prosecution and punishment, is much larger than the discussion of police manipulations. Further, there is a tendency to place the regulation of police manipulations in the hands of the courts.[6] The possibility of a failure of a prosecution is a significant institutional incentive for police. But where the immediate goal of police activity is not prosecution, the possibility of a failure of prosecution will not guide police behaviour. By focusing on 'entrapment' (in its etymologically accurate form), we distract ourselves from the range of possible police manipulations that are available. How should we understand undercover police manipulation in general, and not only the specific case in which police manipulate with the expectation of thereby gaining the grounds to arrest and prosecute the person that is manipulated?

3   On manipulation

If manipulation may be used by police without the immediate goal of a prosecution of the person who is manipulated, then there are really two central questions: (a) when (if at all) can police manipulate? and (b) can people be prosecuted for acts into which they have been manipulated?

For the purposes of the analysis here, I will appeal to Noggle's account of manipulation.[7] Noting that manipulation refers to an apparently disparate set of concepts – 'tempting, inciting, insinuating, conditioning, and playing on emotions'[8] – it is argued that these have in common an attempt to *lead a person astray*. Thus, the view is that 'manipulative action is the attempt to get someone's beliefs, desires, or emotions to violate [the norms that one believes governs them]'.[9] This view has the attraction that it gives a coherent account of these apparently different kinds of phenomena, uniting them in terms that refer to their wrongness.[10] Nonetheless, we might adapt it slightly. Some take the plausible view that manipulation is not itself *prima facie* wrong. Thus, Noggle's position struggles to take account of paternalistic nudges, where people are manipulated into acting in ways that benefit them: in his terms, these appear not to be manipulations at all, as they do not lead astray. But this is an odd result.[11] Here, we can retain Noggle's insight but narrow the scope of his analysis by saying that *wrongful* manipulation is causing someone's beliefs, desires, or emotions to go against what one sees as their best interest.

A related view of manipulation comes in the form of Jeff Howard's argument against 'moral subversion'.[12] This holds that among the features of persons that ground the state's legitimacy are their possession of the two moral powers of being able to do right, and of being able to form and revise a conception of what is good. Leading a person into doing wrong undermines the first of those powers. A challenge to this view is that it is not clear why leading a person to do wrong undermines a person's power to choose between right and wrong any less than leading a person to do right does so. Either way, if we are concerned about the free exercise of a power, it seems to be the *leading* that is objectionable, rather than the place to which the person is led.[13] This problem can be accepted away. Rather than a problem, it is a broadening of the view. Rather than a wrong of moral subversion, we can talk instead about a wrong of manipulating. This will include manipulating people into committing morally neutral or good acts. And indeed, manipulation cannot be wrong just in virtue of the harms it involves. As we noted earlier, there is a debate about the ethics of paternalistic nudges, for example, and this debate occurs in a context in which it is assumed that people are being nudged – that is, manipulated – into performing actions that are good for them.[14] The wrong of manipulation is involved in how people relate to one another and is not limited to the harms it can involve. We might say, then, that the wrong of manipulation is aggravated where it involves procuring a wrongful act, but it is an independent wrong.[15]

4 People can be liable to police manipulation

In accordance with this book's central argument, let us understand the issues around police manipulations in the following terms. It is *prima facie* wrong to manipulate. However, people can forfeit their right against being manipulated, or otherwise become liable to it. Furthermore, sometimes it will be justified to manipulate if the relative consequences of doing so are sufficiently overwhelming. There is a central distinction here between those who are, and are not, *liable* to manipulation. Consider the first category. Can people be liable to *prima facie* wrongful manipulation? In this section I set out cases where they can. In the following section, I discuss police manipulation of the non-liable.

It is not difficult to think of cases in which people can be liable to be killed, imprisoned, restrained, or materially deprived. Perhaps there are some kinds of treatment, such as torture, to which nobody is liable in any circumstances. It is difficult to see why manipulation would fall into this category. Some might see manipulation as particularly disrespectful or autonomy-depriving. The case, however, seems difficult to sustain against the realities of prisons. This case is especially strong if we accept that there is a general deterrence role in the criminal justice system.[16] With general deterrence, people can be liable to be used as a means to the end of preventing other harms against other people. Incarceration is used in order to disincentivise other crimes. If people can be liable to suffer such serious setbacks for a broader crime-preventive goal, it is plausible that they can be liable to these setbacks too.[17]

Suppose that a man has been tracked making sexual advances towards children online. An undercover officer who is trained in mimicking people online takes over the avatar of one of his targets when her parents discover her chat history.[18] The man proposes meeting who he believes is the child in a busy public railway station. It would be difficult to perform an arrest and collect evidence of a planned sexual assault at that location, since the target would be able to flee and discard evidence. The undercover agent posing as the child proposes meeting somewhere quieter, near the back of the railway station. The operations team realise that by proposing a meeting place, they are thereby directing the criminal activity and rendering the operation unlikely to lead to a successful prosecution.

It has become a form of entrapment. Nonetheless, the meeting place is proactively proposed with the goal of disruption of criminality. The target goes to meet the 'child' and is arrested. A prosecution does not take place, but the target is shaken by the experience. In this case, it is difficult to argue that liability to (*prima facie* wrongful) manipulation is absent. The target is threatening a clear public wrong, but the goal is not prosecution.

It may be argued that, on the definition that I am using, this is not wrongful manipulation at all. That definition involves *leading people astray*. In one way, the target is not led astray. Quite the opposite. He is led away from going astray. He is prevented from carrying out a particular very serious wrong and is disrupted in his general efforts at such wrongs. However, even if the operation is a net benefit for the target, it still involves creating beliefs, desires, and attitudes that are contrary to what they should be. The target is led to believe the falsehood that he is to meet a certain kind of person, to expect that he will be able to abuse her, and to become inappropriately excited about doing so. These remain *prima facie* wrongs, and their justification does not lie in their immediate benefit for the target. Showing that one's actions as a whole led a person to a better situation *in comparison to what would otherwise have occurred* is not sufficient to show that one is not wrongfully manipulating them. Suppose the opposite is true. Consider a person who is going to take very serious missteps, to act in ways that are seriously contrary to her interests. Since the baseline is so low, a vast amount of trickery and pressure would be deemed non-wrongful upon her, so long as it leads her to act in ways that are somewhat less mistaken.

The right baseline for understanding *prima facie* wrongful manipulation, then, is what the manipulator could have done, rather than what the target would have done. The point is that *liability* makes the difference in the case described. If we think that the police action in creating the fake meeting is justified, it is because the target is threatening a serious wrong, and has thereby forfeited rights against being manipulated by police. The action is not justified merely because the police action is beneficial to the target.

We can identify other cases where it seems that police can permissibly manipulate a person into committing a wrong. If people can forfeit a right against being manipulated, does it follow that those already involved in criminality can legitimately be manipulated into further criminality? The manipulation of people into criminality can be useful in security terms. For example, an undercover officer makes contact with a person who works on the fringes of a criminal organisation.[19] With an eye to broadening a possible channel of intelligence, the officer encourages this person to become more involved with the group. Depending on considerations of proportionality, the liability view allows this activity, and it is more permissive of this activity in proportion to the gravity of the criminality for which the target was initially culpable.[20]

The position appears to imply, problematically, that there can be a ladder of legitimate manipulations. A person could be liable to a small manipulation into committing a wrong. Committing that wrong makes her liable to a greater manipulation into committing a greater wrong, until she is liable to strong manipulation into committing a terrible wrong. This is not a hypothetical scenario: consider the way that some informants have been used, where they are co-opted into the centre of a criminal network, having, before contact with police, been living only at its periphery.

There are two ways of understanding the issue of ladders of legitimate manipulations. The victim of repeated manipulation either:

(1) commits *all-things-considered justified* acts in each iteration; or
(2) commits *all-things-considered unjustified* acts in each iteration.[21]

According to route (1), it is possible for a person to be liable to manipulation in virtue of having committed an act that is, all things considered, justified. It is doubtful that people can be liable to manipulations in virtue of their committing acts that are justified, all things considered, even if the acts are *prima facie* or *pro tanto* wrongs. However, as we saw in Chapter 4, some views of liability proffer exceptions to this. On such views, where a cost is inevitable and indivisible, the person who is the most responsible bears responsibility for it, even if they are not culpable for it having arisen. In a real case, there will be a point at which we will assign responsibility to police for the outcome of repeated manipulations.

On the other hand according to route (2), it is possible for a person to be justifiably manipulated into an action that is, all things considered, unjustified. It is doubtful that the kinds of acts into which people can be justifiably manipulated are ever all-things-considered wrongs. It is a kind of outsourcing of dirty hands. Suppose that there is some act within a serious organised crime context that would have beneficial consequences, on balance, but is a *pro tanto* wrong. For example, a courier might be encouraged to take a personal risk in photographing some documents. If a state holds that it could not permissibly carry out this act, but could permissibly manipulate a serious criminal into performing it, it opens itself to a charge of hypocrisy. So permissible *prima facie* wrongful manipulations are manipulations into non-wrongful acts, all things considered.

To sum up, I have suggested that there is a range of scenarios in which police can justifiably manipulate people into doing wrong. Where people are liable to such manipulations, they may be punished, but police may also manipulate the liable without the goal of bringing a prosecution, but rather for the purposes of some other policing goal.

5   Police can manipulate the non-liable

Alongside the manipulation of the liable, the framework that I am using suggests that there are possible circumstances in which police are justified in manipulating the non-liable. In particular, they are justified where the consequences of doing so are overwhelmingly positive, according to what I described in the previous chapter as consequentially justified wrongs or lesser evils. There are two kinds of case to consider: small manipulations and serious ones. Consider small manipulations first.

Police manipulations exist where officers generate friendships in order to gain access to their main target. Those on the receiving end of such treatment will sense, on the discovery of the nature of the friendship, that they were wronged in being manipulated. Suppose a police officer befriends the innocent associates of a target, and does so charmingly and in a way that the targets enjoy. This is a form of state-sanctioned manipulation. It leads the targets astray because false friendships are not in people's interests. Even if there is no other discernible harm imposed – suppose that exit is successfully managed socially in a way that does not cause distress – there remains a wrong of manipulation, of people being led and used for some other purpose. Manipulations by undercover police can be *prima facie* wrongs, calling for justification, even when their central purpose is not a criminal or wrongful act by the target.

This is potentially a very powerful result. If the small effects of undercover policing on the non-liable are unjustified, then a great deal of undercover policing will be ruled out, since it will often have these effects. And it will be ruled out from a surprising source: not the large impacts on those targeted, but the small impacts on those who are not targeted.

The lesser evil justification may work in many cases to justify the small manipulations that undercover police deliver upon the non-liable. The disvalue of the small wrongs can be expected to be outweighed by the large crime preventive value of an operation. However, as we saw, this justification leaves in place a complaint on the part of those who are affected. They are thereby entitled to reparations. Police are now construed as being in the position of having very many small compensatory obligations, or of committing further wrongs by failing to meet these obligations.

A better approach involves seeing many of these actions as not evils at all. States impose many setbacks upon citizens in pursuit of general goods. A road is rerouted; a CCTV camera is installed; planning laws are relaxed. In these cases, the central issue is the democratic legitimacy of the action. One cannot assert the rightness of the policy without building on the attitudes and expectations of those who are to be affected. If these policies are put in place, then we only assert rights of reparation if such rights are also a part of a democratic agreement. The ethics of the situation plays into the public discussion, especially in determining the relevant costs and setting out issues of distribution. But there is a wide range of reasonable agreements that can be made with regard to those policies. The small costs of undercover policing upon the non-liable also fall into the category of policy decisions that are best understood as political, rather than ethical, as matters of democratic agreement within a wide range of reasonable outcomes. Thus, I argued in Chapter 2 that small setbacks by undercover police may be justified on the grounds of consent. An ideal undercover policing institution would have democratic legitimacy for the imposition of small costs upon the non-liable, agreed to and justified as a part of membership of a system that provides a broader security benefit. Consent can remove the character of these police actions as wrongful, and thereby removes claims to compensation as a matter of natural law.

How should we deal with larger manipulations upon the non-liable? In these cases, as I argued in Chapter 2, we should have recourse beyond what citizens agree to, because the live issue becomes what citizens *should* agree to. In this case, the only route of justification open is the overwhelming good consequences justification. However, even if such actions might be justified in principle, they will face pragmatic or policy objections. In showing that an action has overwhelming good consequences, one must show that it is overwhelmingly good compared to what else one could have done, as well as overwhelmingly good in comparison to doing nothing.

The framework thus has more restrictive implications than it may first seem. I discussed other extreme harms and pragmatic restrictions upon them in Chapter 3. The framework leaves open the practical possibility of manipulating non-liable people in way that is more than trivial, but less than extreme, where the consequences are overwhelmingly good. An example may be the case of the preacher who devotes personal resources to mentoring someone who turns out to be an undercover police officer who is developing their cover. Again, because it has significant effects on a person who is not liable to this treatment, such an operation would need to overcome a very high justificatory bar, and would (if what I say in Chapter 4 is correct) leave in place obligations of reparation.

6   Limits to police manipulation

There are limits to police manipulation. Central to an assessment of the proportionality of a deployment will be how *beneficial* and how *manipulative* the action is.

Take the benefits first. The proportionality of a deployment will depend on the value that it has in infiltrating a broader group. Those who are culpable for distributing images of child sexual abuse may become liable to manipulation into further such activity, where this would allow police to infiltrate the centre of an organisation that deals in illicit images, because the associated harm is so grave. On the other hand, those who form loose associations with people who are involved in direct action protest and the aggravated trespass offences that typically accompany it are liable to little such treatment, since associating with people who might perform aggravated trespass is not a very serious wrong.

People who are involved in non-serious wrongs may be liable to manipulations, but these manipulations will be proportionate in virtue of the value that they create in the pursuit of a more serious crime. The benefits can lie outside of prosecution or changes in behaviour of the targets themselves, but rather, involve the network in which the target is embedded. Consider again the case of Ray, with which I opened this chapter. The central goal of the manipulation was infiltrative: it was to broaden an investigation, to obtain evidence and intelligence outside of the circle to which Carter had thus far gained access, as well as to obtain evidence against Ray himself. The operation had the benefit that other specific crime is investigated, and also that general deterrence is enhanced through the perception of an effective police force that infiltrates those dealing in weaponry in general. Let us alter the case. Suppose that there was no expectation that a broader criminal group would be infiltrated. Instead of indicating connections to gun suppliers, imagine that the target had indicated the possibility that he himself might be violent, and also that he seemed to be shunned by more serious criminal contacts. There is no evidence that tricking him into proposing serious harm or murder would help to infiltrate any further and thereby disrupt very serious criminal groups. In this case, it may be disproportionate for an undercover officer to go so far as to fake his own arrest in order to contrive a situation in which his target will propose serious harm or murder. The benefits of the operation are vastly diminished.

Alongside the benefits of the action, consider also the degree of manipulativeness. There are different kinds and degrees of manipulative action, varying in how far they play a role in obtaining another to carry out a desired act. We can distinguish between the presentation of an opportunity to do D, the creation of a material cost for a person should they not do D, the provision of a material benefit should they do D, encouragement and praise for doing D, and pressuring, bullying into D. Do we measure wrongful manipulativeness according to the extent of involvement, or also according to the perceived disvalue that is brought about? If I gently nudge a person towards something awful (I make a disparaging remark about his artwork, which is successful and about which he is not only passionate but also insecure and might abandon), is my wrong greater than if I consistently use trickery to cause someone to do something only somewhat against his interests? The answer depends on *how much* trickery is used, and *how awful* the outcome is. The gentle nudge towards something awful is worse than the gentle nudge towards something somewhat bad.

So there are two axes on which we can measure the degree of wrongful manipulation: how far the aimed-at act goes against what one perceives to be in the target's interests, and how far one plays a role in bringing about this act. We might say that the limits to police manipulation depend on how wrongfully manipulative an act is, and not just on how manipulative it is.

There is a further aggravating factor in manipulation, which is that we tend to assign greater wrong to manipulations of citizens by state agents. Sarah Buss argues that manipulation and deception are woven into our social norms and practices.[22] Consider, for example, the deceptions and manipulations that take place in early romantic love. Direct honesty is often not a virtue in this circumstance, and also the behaviours surrounding early romantic love are not fraught with wrongs, and indeed are a part of a normal good life.[23] The undercover officer's romantic deceptions and manipulations, on the other hand, are aggravated by the fact that he acts as a state agent; the lie is materially central to the relationship.

We have seen in this section, then, how the specifics of understanding limits on manipulations depend on a close accounting of their benefits and harms.

7 Stings

So far in this chapter I have focused on the *infiltrative* paradigm of undercover policing. In this section I will turn to *the sting*. This involves leading people to carry out and act with the goal of securing a successful prosecution for that act. Can people be punished for acts into which the state has manipulated them? This is not a book about punishment; nonetheless, consider how some of the arguments about entrapment interact with the view that I have put forward.

Some argue that entrapment is *incoherent*. The purpose of the police is to prevent crime and police causing crime is the opposite.[24] If this argument is correct, then it provides an extra layer on top of what I have argued so far in this chapter. Police manipulation is far more restricted than I have suggested, as police can never act in a way that leads to more immediate crime, even if they do so in the expectation that their actions will lead to less crime overall. However, as Hill et al. argue, the incoherence objection to entrapment appears to depend on an extremely strong presupposition, 'a strong Kantian-style premise to the effect that *the end of preventing crime* can never be suspended in the short term for the sake of greater realization in the long term'.[25] That premise seems difficult to defend.

Instead of focusing on the coherence of police action, some argue that when people are entrapped, they are not liable to punishment, because by pressing people's psychological levers, people are no longer responsible and so no longer culpable for their actions. Paul Hughes argues, 'strong temptations will compromise and, in cases of irresistible temptation, undermine the autonomy of those subject to them'.[26] This argument notoriously faces the challenge of explaining why it makes a strong difference for police to urge people into crime, in comparison to mere citizens. Most would not take the view that people are wrongfully entrapped when other citizens tempt a them in to crime. In any case, suppose that a version of this argument succeeds.[27] If so, we can separate the question of what treatment people make themselves liable to, from the question of what treatment the police or the state may impose upon people. So it is theoretically open that people may permissibly be manipulated without being liable to punishment for the act that they committed while being manipulated. Absence of the right kind of autonomy would provide one such ground.[28] It is possible, then, for it to be legitimate for police to manipulate a person into committing a wrong, but at the same time for it to be illegitimate for the state to punish on the grounds of that act into which the person was manipulated. This is the case even if the person was liable to be manipulated.

So let us put the caveat in place that the legitimacy of punishment will ultimately depend on factors beyond police action; for the purposes of the discussion here, I will allow that people can be punished for acts into which they are liable to be manipulated.[29] Consider the nature of stings. Wachtel provides a helpful classification according to (a) how *authentic* or *inauthentic* the opportunity to commit a crime is, and (b) how *focused* or *diffuse* the targeting of the sting is.[30] These two distinctions yield four broad areas of types of sting. A fully authentic opportunity is one that the target would have faced anyhow. A fully targeted sting is aimed at a person against whom there is already strong evidence that they are involved in wrongdoing and are likely to take the bait. Both factors are a matter of degree. On the face of things, targeted and authentic stings are the least problematic, as they respond to existing suspicions and do not present artificial opportunities. A diffuse, authentic sting might be a decoy pickpocket mark, although this would be more targeted if it is deployed in an area in which it is known that pickpockets operate and may be less authentic if it is made into an easier apparent opportunity. A focused, inauthentic sting might involve selling certain stolen goods to a known target, although this would be somewhat authentic insofar as the target could be expected to come across similar opportunities.

In the light of what I have argued in this chapter, I suggest that we can build on this classification. Aside from authenticity, I have argued that we should measure the degree of manipulativeness of an action not just according to how much pressure and trickery is involved but also according to how far the target is led astray. Manipulation into an act that is more wrongful is more manipulative. Thus, in assessing stings, a related category to authenticity is how wrongful the act that a person is led to commit, and we can talk of *manipulativeness*, whereby inauthenticity is an element of manipulativeness.

Furthermore, targeting is a relevant factor, but the grounds on which the targeting is carried out is the key issue. Targeting can occur on the basis of evidence or intelligence that those targeted are likely to take the bait of the sting. It can also occur on the grounds that it is expected that the sting will have significant benefits. Liability and benefit will tend to run together: a successful sting will tend to be a more beneficial one in security terms. But the two factors can separate. There could be a case where the crime is extremely serious and urgent, and in which a person is target even though evidence of his liability is relatively weak. And it could be that there is strong evidence that a certain person is liable, but only for a very small crime – as with stings for possession of small quantities of low grade drugs. We can talk of focused and diffusely targeted stings, therefore, keeping in mind that our assessment should depend on the reasons behind the targeting structure.

Consider a regime of test purchasing of alcohol and tobacco, aiming to check whether vendors will sell to those who are underage.

The practice is fairly diffuse and somewhat beneficial and, let us suppose, is guided by evidence that some vendors will sell to the underage. The opportunities are authentic insofar as they mimic real attempts by children to purchase these goods. Similarly, consider the use of decoys deployed in an area known for pickpocketing. This is also fairly diffuse and beneficial, and may be reasonably authentic.

It might be argued that the framework I am putting forward implies that virtue testing of citizens should be vastly expanded. According to this argument, those who are not caught by stings undergo some cost, in having some time wasted at a purchase, or in having another person standing in their way in a busy shopping street, but these are not serious costs. On the other hand, those who are caught by the sting undergo a more serious manipulation, as they are led to carry out an attempt to commit a crime, but they are, it seems *ex post* liable to this treatment, since they were willing to commit the crime. In this case, the practice of test purchases and decoys is not at all objectionable and should be subject to few limits. This is especially so if it is the case, as I suggest earlier, that people consent to, and thereby do not have a complaint against, small setbacks imposed by undercover police, such as the small setbacks associated with stings in which the bait is not taken up, or having people blocking one's way in the street.

This result contrasts with our attitude towards random virtue testing, which is, for example, explicitly prohibited in UK and Canadian case law.[31] However, even assuming that only idealised authentic opportunities are presented in each case, the argument overstates the point for four reasons. First, vastly enlarged test purchase or decoy regimes would present an inauthentic *number* of opportunities to commit crime, and in that way would be far more manipulative. Second, if the regime does not have real democratic support among the group who suffer the costs, then the argument of consent will fall. Third, as we will see in Chapter 6, these costs may be larger than they first appear, as they include broader chilling effects upon people's actions. The legitimacy of these deployments, then, will depend on these contextual specifics. Fourth, it does not follow from the fact that a person has succumbed to a sting that they were liable to any manipulation. A person is not threatening a wrong, just because, counterfactually, they would commit a wrong in a particular circumstance. If so, there is a higher bar to show liability than the fact that a person has taken the bait in a sting.

Consider another pair of cases.[32] First:

> suppose that a series of violent rapes have been occurring in a public park, ones for which the authorities have no identified suspects. The authorities could actively surveil the park in an attempt to catch the perpetrator in the act. Yet the park might be large and the perpetrator's acts intermittent. So instead of 'watching and waiting', the authorities hatch a scheme to send an armed undercover female agent into the park at night to see if they can lure the perpetrator into an attack.[33]

In this case, the targeting is somewhat diffuse, aimed at a geographic area, with a very high possible benefit. The target presents an authentic situation, a woman walking in a park. Second, consider the practice of using internet stings against paedophiles, whereby police place classified adverts online offering sex with a minor. Police pose as a child, arrange meetings with any who make contact, and arrest those who show up.[34] These operations are fairly diffuse. Insofar as there is evidence that those who respond to such adverts are or would be involved in child sexual abuse, they are less diffuse and more targeted. If so, the benefit is high, and the opportunity may be authentic. It looks at first, then, that these two operations, the agent in the park and the classified advert sting, are on a par. Lippke notes that it is unclear, in fact, in the latter case, whether there was prior evidence that any people had intention to commit sexual assaults on minors. However, once arrests have been made, it appears that there is such evidence, and stings of this kind continue to yield successful prosecutions. There are other empirical considerations that would distinguish the two operations. It may be that those who fall for these stings are a different category to those who abuse children, because the stings are highly inauthentic; one assessment of the evidence urges, 'The phrase "foolish, old man" comes to mind much more readily than "dangerous criminal"'.[35] If this is correct, then the manipulation involved is heavy and the benefit diminished.

Consider one final example. Imagine a person who had promised to supply an undercover officer a certain quantity of contraband. At the subsequent meeting, the target states that he is now only able to

supply half the proposed amount. Acting in role, the undercover officer expresses strong frustration and demands that the original plan
is followed. He would be surprised if his expressed frustration made
any difference: the target has been clear that he can no longer supply
the full amount, and sudden breaks in supply are common. In this
milieu, it is also normal to communicate forcefully when such breaks
occur. Had the officer not acted in role, suspicions may have arisen in
the target and the deal may have fallen through altogether. The target
has now been encouraged by the state to break the law. Specifically,
to do double what he might have done. The target eventually supplies
the diminished amount to the officer and is arrested for doing so. In
this case, the target is encouraged to supply more contraband only
so that it is more certain that he will supply what he has promised
to supply. The manipulation involves continued encouragement to
carry out this action.[36]

Is the target liable to the manipulation? There are two key moments
to consider. First is at the initial agreement to supply. Second is at the
moment at which the target is actively encouraged to supply double
what he can. At both moments, we would want to know whether
there is reason to think that the target is a threat. At the first, we
may be more hesitant to think so, since less intelligence has been
gathered upon the target. But also in the first moment, it seems from
the case that less manipulation is applied. The relatively low level
of manipulation in a test buy may be justified, given significant benefits in preventing serious crime.[37] At the second moment, far more
is known, and also, more manipulation is applied. Again it seems
implausible to rule the police actions out as illegitimate, depending
on the size of the values at stake.

Taking these cases together, we can see how there is a range of
factors playing into whether a sting is permissible. I have focused on
how targeted the sting is (noting that the grounds for targeting can
appeal both to the target's liability and to the benefits of the operation) and how manipulative it is (wherein manipulativeness refers
both to the authenticity of the opportunity and the seriousness of the
act that is elicited). My view of police manipulation locates entrapment within the broader context of undercover policing that includes
infiltration as well as sting activities. This is important, because a
great deal of infiltration work will involve manipulating people into
carrying out morally neutral acts: having a conversation, making a

friend, and so forth. I have proposed that we should find *even these* comparatively innocuous acts by undercover police as worthy of close regulative attention. On the other hand, entrapment, even as it is classically understood, might be justified in some circumstances, where there is liability and strong benefit in disrupting crime.

Notes

1 Carter, Joe. Undercover. London: Arrow Books, 2017.
2 Lewis, Paul, and Rob Evans. Undercover: The True Story of Britain's Secret Police. London: Guardian Faber Publishing, 2014.
3 Innes, Martin, and James W. E. Sheptycki. 'From Detection to Disruption'. International Criminal Justice Review 14, no. 1 (2004): 1–24.
4 As described in the memoir by Marcus, Tom. Soldier Spy. London: Penguin, 2017.
5 This may be understood as a person's declared interests or purposes, or their interests and purposes understood objectively.
6 Walker, Clive, and Kingsley Hyland. 'Undercover Policing and Underwhelming Laws'. Criminal Law Review 8 (21 March 2014). We return to this topic in chapter 6.
7 Noggle, Robert. 'Manipulative Actions: A Conceptual and Moral Analysis'. American Philosophical Quarterly 33, no. 1 (1996): 43–55.
8 Ibid., p. 44.
9 Ibid.
10 Compare Moti Gorin, who offers an argument that manipulation involves trafficking in reasons, but that these can still be good reasons. On this understanding, merely by concealing their goals and status, undercover officers engage in manipulation in every interaction that they have, while they are acting undercover, even those interactions that involve offering good reasons and are directly beneficial. (Gorin, Moti. 'Do Manipulators Always Threaten Rationality?' American Philosophical Quarterly 51, no. 1 (2014a).) One might square the two accounts by arguing that manipulation always involves deception, because it involves dissembling about one's intentions (Bělohrad, Radim. 'The Nature and Moral Status of Manipulation'. Acta Analytica 34, no. 4 (2019).
11 Noggle replies to such concerns by arguing that paternalistic nudges that emphasise the salience of one particular class of reasons are manipulative if they 'increase the salience so that it is disproportionate to that fact's true relevance and importance for the decision at hand'. ('Manipulation, Salience, and Nudges'. Bioethics 32, no. 3 (2018): 164–70). This seems to be a departure, however from the view initially stated. Consistently building on the original view, one can hold that salience nudges are manipulative if they are expected to lead a person to act so that the factor is given disproportionate weight. That is, the view is concerned with actually leading people astray, not with representing an improper

balance of reasons to them. If so, then misrepresenting the proper balance of reasons in a way that does not lead a person astray, as with paternalistic manipulation, is not manipulative. And this seems to be an incorrect analysis. Rather, we should allow a category of non-wrongful manipulation.

12 Howard, Jeffrey W. 'Moral Subversion and Structural Entrapment'. Journal of Political Philosophy (1 August 2015).

13 For a version of this challenge see Stanhope, Jonathan. 'Against Jeffrey Howard on Entrapment'. Journal of Ethics and Social Philosophy 15 (2019): 283.

14 Wilkinson argues that it can be permissible to counter-manipulate people into actions that are in their own interests in contexts in which they are being manipulated against their own interests. For example, appeals to the effects upon men's virility of tobacco may be permissible against a background of adverts containing smoking cowboys. (Wilkinson, T. Martin. 'Counter-Manipulation and Health Promotion'. Public Health Ethics 10, no. 3 (2017): 257–66).

15 A note on the dialectic. I am asserting an independent *prima facie* wrong of manipulation, and that is enough for the ensuing discussion. I have not grounded or given a theory of this wrong, although I have given reason to think that it is a specific kind of wrong. My approach is ecumenical. On the substantive philosophical question of the explanation of the wrong of manipulation, many argue that it is wrongful because it interferes with people's autonomy. For this and a defence of the opposing view, see Buss, Sarah. 'Valuing Autonomy and Respecting Persons: Manipulation, Seduction, and the Basis of Moral Constraints'. Ethics 115, no. 2 (2005): 195–235.

16 I leave open the response that punishment is, on the whole, not justified. C.f. Boonin, David. The Problem of Punishment. Cambridge and New York: Cambridge University Press, 2008.

17 Some will resist this line of reasoning by arguing that setbacks imposed by the courts have a very different status to setbacks imposed by the police. However, as I argue elsewhere, it is harder than it first appears to sustain such a distinction (Nathan, Christopher. 'Principles of Policing and Principles of Punishment'. Legal Theory 22, nos. 3–4 (December 2016): 181–204). If the reader still finds the point in this paragraph unpersuasive, consider instead the idea that a person can make himself, through his own behaviour, liable to the setbacks involved in arrest and pre-trial detention.

18 For discussion of this kind of police operation, see Grant, Tim, and Nicci MacLeod. Language and Online Identities: The Undercover Policing of Internet Sexual Crime. Cambridge and New York, NY: Cambridge University Press, 2020. In defence of the kinds of laws behind this type of operation, see Sorell, Tom. 'Online Grooming and Preventive Justice'. Criminal Law and Philosophy (27 June 2016): 1–20.

19 Joh, Elizabeth E. 'Breaking the Law to Enforce It: Undercover Police Participation in Crime'. Stanford Law Review 62 (2009): 46.

20 In reality, it appears that there is a tendency for such people to be swept up in prosecutions, if they are not classed as informants. This is a contingent fact. There need not be the goal of obtaining a prosecution for that act.

21 One could imagine a case that combines the two, in which case both of the arguments put below would apply.

22 Buss, Sarah. 'Valuing Autonomy and Respecting Persons: Manipulation, Seduction, and the Basis of Moral Constraints'. Ethics 115, no. 2 (2005): 195–235.

23 For accounts of what secrets are and are not permissible in sexual relations, see Dougherty, Tom. 'Sex, Lies, and Consent'. Ethics (17 July 2015); Lazenby, Hugh, and Iason Gabriel. 'Permissible Secrets'. The Philosophical Quarterly 68, no. 271 (1 April 2018): 265–85.

24 Dworkin, Gerald. 'The Serpent Beguiled Me and I Did Eat: Entrapment and the Creation of Crime'. Law and Philosophy 4, no. 1 (1985): 17–39; Ashworth, Andrew. 'What Is Wrong with Entrapment'. Singapore Journal of Legal Studies 1999 (1999): 293.

25 Hill, Daniel, Stephen McLeod, and Attila Tanyi. 'What Is the Incoherence Objection to Legal Entrapment?' Available at SSRN 3337625, 2019, p. 34 https://papers.ssrn.com/sol3/papers.cfm?abstract_id=3337625 (accessed May 2021).

26 Hughes, Paul M. 'What Is Wrong with Entrapment?' The Southern Journal of Philosophy 42, no. 1 (1 March 2004): 58.

27 For example, Hochan Kim argues that the wrong of entrapment lies in *illegetimate* interference with autonomy. 'Entrapment, Culpability, and Legitimacy'. Law and Philosophy 39, no. 1 (1 February 2020): 67–91.

28 Another would be considerations of fairness. Dilloff, Anthony M. 'Unraveling Unlawful Entrapment'. J. Crim. L. & Criminology 94 (2003): 827.

29 Alternatively, stings may be deployed with a disruptive intent, aiming to shake up the target, as described earlier in this chapter. This may apply even where it is not expected that a prosecution will succeed.

30 Wachtel, Julius. 'From Morals to Practice: Dilemmas of Control in Undercover Policing'. Crime, Law and Social Change 18, nos. 1–2 (1992): 137–58.

31 R v Loosely, R. v. Barnes 1991 1 S.C.R. 449.

32 These are put forward and compared in Lippke, Richard L. 'A Limited Defense of What Some Will Regard as Entrapment'. Legal Theory 23, no. 4 (2017): 283–306.

33 Lippke, Richard L. 'A Limited Defense of What Some Will Regard as Entrapment'. Legal Theory 23, no. 4 (2017): 303.

34 Peter Holley, Fla. 'Child Sex Sting Nabs 22 Suspects, Including Methodist Pastor Who Volunteered in Schools'. Wash. Post, 16 September 2016. www.washingtonpost.com/news/true-crime/wp/2016/09/16/fla-child-sex-sting-nets-22-men-including-youth-pastor-who-volunteered-in-schools/ (accessed May 2021).

35 Fulda, J. S. 'Internet Stings Directed at Pedophiles: A Study in Philosophy and Law'. Sexuality & Culture 11, no. 1(2007): 60.
36 Drawing on Carter, Joe. London: Arrow Books, 2017.
37 This is notwithstanding the note on the nature of the 'war on drugs', as discussed in chapter 1.

6   Oversight

1   Introduction

In this chapter I discuss the policy implications of what I have argued. First, I examine the idea that undercover police may engage in crimes, and suggest how this can be made compatible with the rule of law. Second, I consider how the overall effects of undercover policing give reason to oversee its effects centrally. Third, I argue that because judgments of liability of those affected are a central part of assessing whether an undercover operation is proportionate, there should be judicial involvement in authorisations.

2   Otherwise illegal activity and the rule of law

It can be useful, in policing terms, for undercover officers to commit crimes. It is useful because it provides a way for officers to maintain or build their cover. Infiltrations may be impossible without these acts. Should such state criminality be permitted? 'State criminality' is a misnomer if there is a legal basis for the acts. In the UK, the Covert Human Intelligence Sources Act (2021) provides a legal basis for undercover police to commit otherwise illegal acts.

Opposition to the act has arisen partly on the grounds that permitting a class of state actors to engage in illegal acts runs counter to the rule of law.[1] The *rule of law objection* holds that even *otherwise* illegal acts by state agents are in conflict with the rule of law. In his discussion of the grounds of policing, Luke William Hunt offers an argument of this sort, and, further, provides a powerful development of it in order to understand the proper limits of policing.[2] Hunt argues

DOI: 10.4324/9780429293443-6

that the central issue with police stings is that they involve the police committing acts that are otherwise illegal. Were ordinary citizens to purchase contraband or to incite people to violence, they would be committing criminal acts. Stings involve acts by state agents that would be illegal, except for the special circumstances in which they are authorised.

For Hunt, the problem with otherwise illegal acts is that these exceptions can be inconsistent with the rule of law. We value being governed by laws and not merely the discretion of those with power. Imagine a category of state agents was given a blanket exception to some criminal statute. This would be inconsistent with the substantive value of the rule of law, of government by laws and not by people. That value is manifested only when laws apply to all and are not gerrymandered to give special exceptions or executive authority to some individuals.

When *can* the state engage in otherwise illegal acts, in line with the rule of law? Drawing on Locke, Hunt gives four necessary conditions: the power is used for public good; the legislature could not act in time; there is much at stake (such as in cases of national security or terrorism); and the power is not an 'affront to liberal personhood'.[3] These are the kinds of extreme circumstance in which our attachment to the rule of law can be overcome by other important goods.

Hunt defines stings as involving otherwise illegal activity.[4] However, stings need not involve otherwise illegal activity, according to their normal definition. A more orthodox definition of a sting involves the creation of an apparent criminal opportunity, with the goal of obtaining evidence of the target seeking to engage in that opportunity. The creation of a criminal opportunity is not necessary illegal. The relevant otherwise illegal act alluded to is a double inchoate crime: an incitement on the part of the officer to an attempt on the part of the target at a criminal act. Incitement in the UK (now called 'encouraging or assisting a crime') requires an intention that a crime occur, or at least, a belief that an offence will occur.[5] It is questionable whether this *mens rea* is properly present in the case of the sting. Where police set up a system of virtue testing, they could be construed as only intending that those who do commit crimes are apprehended, rather than as intending that crimes are committed, and where the system of virtue testing is sufficiently broad, the expectation that an offence will occur in any one test may be absent.

Assuming that we accept Hunt's stringent conditions on legitimate otherwise-illegal acts by state actors, the 'rule of law' argument requires an account of what counts as an otherwise illegal act (OIA). We can have a law that states that officers acting to procure crimes in the course of stings are not acting unlawfully. If that law gains democratic assent, then sting officers are not engaged in OIAs, any more than chopping vegetables is an OIA that would be unlawful were there a person under one's knife rather than a carrot. A legal code might be constructed so that each individual crime is set forth with an exception where it is used in stings. Or police authorised otherwise-criminal activity may be written as a defence, alongside other defences in law. These possibilities show that we cannot lean on the structure of the law in understanding the 'otherwise illegal' view. We do not say that a person who commits all but one of the defined elements of a crime has committed an otherwise illegal act; she has not committed a crime at all. Or if it is otherwise illegal, there is no question of the rule of law being infringed upon in finding her not guilty. Similarly, we could say that a person who successfully upholds a defence against a charge has acted otherwise illegally, but, once again, this is not to invoke the idea that the rule of law has not applied in this case. To develop the view, we need to be able to draw out why authorised police acts that are otherwise criminal are relevantly different. With the bare idea of otherwise illegal acts, aside from the idea that *some* authorisations of otherwise illegal acts by state agents infringes upon the rule of law, we are left in the dark about *which*.

Thus, Hunt argues that the rule of law includes not just the idea that government follows the law, but that the rule of law also contains *principles*, in particular, 'principles that might oppose vast legal authority for any tactics the government sees fit to authorize'.[6] Many do, indeed, see the rule of law as something that makes sense only if it is taken to incorporate substantive principles.[7] However, there is another, influential, way of seeing the rule of law. This is to understand it as a virtue of law, and not necessarily as a virtue in general. Joseph Raz argues:

> the rule of law is just one of the virtues which a legal system may possess and by which it is to be judged. It is not to be confused with democracy, justice, equality (before the law or

otherwise), human rights of any kind or respect for persons or for the dignity of man. A non-democratic legal system, based on the denial of human rights, on extensive poverty, on racial seg-regation, sexual inequalities, and religious persecution may, in principle, conform to the requirements of the rule of law better than any of the legal systems of the more enlightened Western democracies. This does not mean that it will be better than those Western democracies. It will be an immeasurably worse legal system, but it will excel in one respect: in its conformity to the rule of law.[8]

In this spirit, Jeremy Waldron expresses the concern that there is a tendency to build into the rule of law whatever one sees as important substantively correct laws, complaining in particular about the view that laws that conflict with property rights or economic liberty are inconsistent with the rule of law. Once one steps beyond the bounds of the rule of law as a virtue of law, and into the area of substantive values, it is hard to resist a 'free for all', in which the rule of law loses its meaning because it is only met when the speaker's own values are met by a system of law.[9]

There is a danger, then, in building a case from the value of the rule of law, to the conclusion that otherwise illegal activity by under-cover police should be severely restricted. This is that in order to make this argument, we depend upon a contested conception of the rule of law, and it is unclear what resources one can appeal to in order to resolve disagreement about this, except the very same resources that we have before resort to that discussion. A more fruitful version of the *rule of law argument* focuses on the formal elements of the rule of law, elements that one will subscribe to whether or not one commits to a substantive view of the concept. Although Hunt con-trasts the Razian view of the rule of law with the view that the rule of law involves principles, it should be emphasised that Raz also argues that the rule of law is built from a set of principles, though these are formal rather than substantive. Raz offers an incomplete list of such principles: laws are prospective, open, clear, and stable; law-making is guided by rules; the judiciary is independent and the courts have powers of review; the principles of natural justice are observed; the courts are easily accessible; and the 'discretion of the crime-preventing agencies should not be allowed to pervert the law'.[10]

This last is illustrated with the case of prosecutors choosing not to prosecute certain crimes or certain classes of offenders.

It may be possible to draw upon the insight behind this last principle in order to build an account of otherwise illegal police action. The issue is not just that the acts would be illegal. It is that they are carried out with wide discretion. Of the recent Act in the UK, one commentator argues that the authorisations for undercover operations involving otherwise criminal conduct should not remain within police force:

> Surely the rule of law at least demands that decisions to authorise serious criminal activity not be left solely to police officers (or other officials), even if they have attained a particular rank, and certainly not in the huge range of agencies covered by this bill.[11]

Similarly, Clive Walker argues that the Act has a number of benefits.

> [It] legalizes wrongdoing by an authorized [undercover officer or informant], rather than leaving claims to immunity as uncertain general legal defenses such as duress or self-defense. . . . In terms of the rule of law, the Bill can be welcomed as a 'belated recognition that regulating the permitted conduct of CHIS must be set up by a formal legislative footing' in accordance with the rule of law as legality.[12]

However, it also has a serious flaw:

> the Bill's grant of impunity negates the notion of the rule of law as equality and does so for an especially dangerous activity where oversight and accountability are inherently difficult to secure.[13]

So, even the Razian rule of law may be threatened by the UK Act, as that Act does not provide for proper oversight but rather permits 'impunity' on the part of law enforcement. It is of especial concern that it provides authorisation powers to such a wide range of agencies. The Act formalises powers not only with the police and intelligence services but also other branches of government, including HM Revenue and Customs and the Food Standards Agency.

Furthermore, the power to act illegally can be invoked on broad grounds, such as the prevention of disorder. Many will take the view that this is too wide a power without sufficient oversight across arms of government. It thereby comes into conflict with the last of Raz's principles for the rule of law.

Rather than focusing on the rhetoric of the rule of law, I would suggest that the key issues in this topic relate to accountability and judgments of harms, and to the creation of governance systems that are most likely to make the proper judgments. Otherwise-criminal acts can be expected to heighten several of the harms of undercover policing. They are likely to involve causing harms directly; they may increase the risk of psychological harm to officers; they may decrease trust in the criminal justice system; they may encourage others to commit crime. In her discussion of law breaking by law enforcement, Elizabeth Joh argues, 'The simple absence of transparency in police decisionmaking can be destructive, both in its potential to breed police abuse as well as to foment public distrust'.[14] She advocates some basic regulations: reporting of numbers, regulatory guidelines, more research. In the case of otherwise-criminal acts, institutions can be set up in ways that make transparency professionally risky for individuals, where the decisions to be made can be troubling or psychologically corrupting, and where the factors that need to be taken into account in order to judge properly the proportionality of an operation involve ethical judgments about responsibility. We should hold in the foreground the challenge of setting up institutions that are likely to make such judgments in a trustworthy manner.

Importantly, alongside these concerns, and in contrast to the objection from the rule of law, it remains open that we might construct a regulative system that has the virtue of the UK Act – that it puts otherwise-criminal acts by undercover officers on a legislative footing – and also avoids its vice, by implementing a robust system of external governance.

3   General oversight and macro-proportionality

In this section, I suggest that there are two central reasons for centralised oversight of undercover policing. First, alongside the harms and setbacks that it can impose on specific individuals collaterally, undercover policing also has a series of generalised costs. Second, there is a possible problem of macro-disproportionality.

Undercover policing can have a *chilling effect* on public discourse. For example:

> The FBI contacted a suspect online with a link to a fake news story about the threats, purportedly by the Associated Press. The link contained hidden spyware that enabled the FBI to locate and eventually arrest 15-year-old Josh Glazebrook. The CEO of the Associated Press argued that in 'stealing our identity', the FBI 'corrode[d] the most fundamental tenet of a free press – our independence from government control'.[15]

Here, the effect upon the trustworthiness of the media is an element of a broader effect on the ability of civil society to converse. Similarly, it is often proposed that people behave differently when they believe that they may be being watched.[16] They will be more circumspect, less likely to deviate from mainstream norms or even to express ideas that run contrary to the mainstream. The mere suggestion that an authority is aware of their behaviour will alter people's behaviour; it is inhibiting. This is a way in which intrusive policing – whether carried out by undercover officers, surveillance, or informants – can operate subtly to undermine people's freedom.

There also is a difficult-to-evidence but plausible thesis that the legitimation of normally immoral behaviour by the police has deleterious effects on the *norms of law enforcement*. In the context of a discussion of police deception in general, Jerome Skolnick notes that police act in deceptive ways as a matter of course in their investigations, for example, in the use of informants and test buys, and he puts forward the hypothesis that 'Judicial acceptance of deception in the investigation process enhances moral acceptance of deception by detectives in the interrogatory and testimonial stages of criminal investigation, and thus increases the probability of its occurrence'.[17] That is to say, the general practice of deception in some spheres is likely to lead to it being carried out in others. This leakage occurs through the way in which the justification for deception typically occurs at the investigative stage of the criminal process: 'When detectives deceive suspects in the course of criminal investigations or interrogations . . . [t]he end of truth justifies for the modern detective the means of lying.'[18] The empirical claim is admittedly speculative, if highly plausible.[19] The idea behind it is that by fostering the consequentialist reasoning that justifies deceptions on the grounds that they reveal more important truths, one desensitises a person to the non-consequentialist norm against lying, and thereby encourages such activity in other parts of their life, fostering a 'subcultural norm' of police perjury,[20] in which police will testify falsehoods so as to cover up the corruption of other police officers which, if revealed, would cause a trial to collapse.

Apart from possible corruptive effects upon the criminal justice system that follow from the proliferation of authorised deceptive and manipulative police activity, there are also challenges for the institution of policing itself. By creating a professional sub-unit that is dedicated to the art of deploying social skills that in any other context would be considered wrongful, the practice can have the effect of undermining cohesion within the police force. Thus, Bethan Loftus states one of the findings of her study of undercover policing within the UK as follows:

> Certain key features of covert police working life – for instance, the normalized necessity to lie to people and engage in scenarios that lure people into committing crime – are particularly tainting. Within the organization, covert officers operate on the fringes, are resented by their uniformed colleagues and live in a heightened sense of anxiety for fear about revealing their identity. While they collate what can be significant evidence or intelligence about criminal activity, they are nevertheless exempt from experiencing the prestige for their contribution.[21]

The tendency towards separation and institutional isolation that undercover work seems to encourage is illustrated at its most extreme by the Special Demonstration Squad, and later the National Public Order Information Unit. While these were official elements of the Metropolitan Police, they acted somewhat autonomously and with a lack of oversight, and tend to be quickly disowned by other police officers.[22]

All of these costs – chilling effects, effects on the norms of law enforcement, effects on law enforcement practices – mean that there is strong reason to assess the proportionality of undercover policing taken as a whole, as well as the proportionality of individual under-cover policing operations. A question in practice for strategic assessments of the use of undercover policing is how far these effects are in operation, how effectively they are mitigated – and also, if they are unavoidable or avoidable only at great cost, how far we should be willing to accept these harms and setbacks for the sake of the benefits of proactive policing.

There is a further reason for central authorisation. In order to retain overall proportionality, it is important to preempt the problem of multiple targeting, whereby the normal structure of the intelligence ladder will make it possible that several different operations affecting the same individual will seem to be individually proportionate. Taken in isolation these may seem justified, but taken as a bundle it is possible that an individual is treated disproportionately, by suffering from being the target of repeated, or even multiple concurrent, operations. Once a person has been a target, police will hold information about them, and they are thereby a cheaper and less risky target than others. Nonetheless, having been the target of an undercover operation, a person who has posed no new threat may be less liable, other things, equal, to serious intrusion. If principle is to be honoured, then it will be necessary to have oversight not just of each undercover operation and its effects, but of the practice of undercover policing (and indeed, seriously intrusive policing) in general, and its effects as a structure upon individuals.

Accordingly, the establishment in the UK of the Investigatory Powers Commissioner's Office by the 2016 Investigatory Powers Act is a positive step. This body is responsible for overseeing all covert investigatory powers. This contrasts with the approach in the United States, where regulation takes place through the exclusion of prohibited acts, rather than through the positive authorisation of an operation, using what Harfield describes as a 'negative liberty model'.[23]

4   An argument for judicial involvement

4.1   *Existing structures*

In this section I argue, focusing on the UK case, that existing governance structures do not expressly take on the idea that undercover police operations should be sensitive to people's liability, even if they do so indirectly or informally. The framework that I have put forward thereby gives a reason in favour of judicial authorisation of operations.

The UK regime draws on European Convention on Human Rights concepts of necessity and proportionality. Surprisingly, this governance framework appears not to demand explicit consideration of evidence of actual or expected wrongdoing of those targeted in authorising intrusions. The law on investigatory powers designates some intrusions upon the non-culpable as proportionate. Intrusions should be proportionate to 'what is sought to be achieved'. That can be national security or the prevention or detection of crime.[24] Taken on its face, this concept is independent of the culpability of the targets for the state of affairs that makes them useful as targets of covert investigations. As one author summarises the position, this is an exercise in balancing 'the nature and extent of the interference against the reasons for interfering'.[25] Suppose an intrusion upon a particular individual is proposed. The intrusion has the goal of gathering information as part of investigation into a national security threat. Does it matter to the proportionality of the intrusion whether the target is in any way implicated in the threat to national security? The answer, according to the UK's Regulation of Investigatory Powers Act (2000) (RIPA) seems to be, strictly, 'no' – or at least, 'not directly': those making judgments of proportionality are asked to balancing only the values of what is sought to be achieved, and the harm or interference to be imposed in achieving this.

The structure does demand extra consideration in assessments of proportionality for those who are not the *targets* of an investigation. There are requirements in the Codes of Practice that accompany RIPA (though not in the Act itself) that 'collateral intrusion' is taken into account.[26] Collateral intrusions are intrusions upon those who are not the subject of the intended investigation; that is, upon those who are perceived to be irrelevant. Those who are perceived to be innocent and relevant are to be treated according to the same standard of proportionality as those who are considered relevant and are under suspicion. This is explicit in the rules covering informants and undercover operations. The August 2018 *Revised Code of Practice on Covert Human Intelligence Sources §3.12* repeats the guidance of previous Codes in stating:

> Where [informant or undercover police] activity is deliberately proposed against individuals who are not suspected of direct or culpable involvement in the matter being investigated, interference with the private and family life of such individuals should not be considered as collateral intrusion but rather as intended intrusion. Any such interference should be carefully considered against the necessity and proportionality criteria as described above.

Those criteria referred to in the last sentence involve 'balancing the seriousness of the intrusion into the private or family life of the subject of the operation (or any other person who may be affected) against the need for the activity in investigative and operational terms' (ibid., §3.3). That is, where it is proposed that a target should be intruded upon (presumably on the grounds that such an intrusion upon the target is expected to yield information relevant to the investigation), then regardless of innocence or suspected guilt, considerations of proportionality are to be made by comparing not only the harm and the benefit but also the culpability or responsibility of the target.[27]

   Some have taken a requirement that collateral intrusions should be considered as sufficient protection for those who are not under suspicion, and seemingly do so by conflating the category of those who are innocent with the category of those who are irrelevant. The 2015 report of the Investigatory Powers Review, 'A Question of Trust', describes the intrusion regime in the following terms:

> Measures taken must be proportionate to the objective, meaning that the measure must be selected that least restricts human rights and that special care is taken to minimise the adverse impact of any measures on the rights of individuals, including *in particular persons who are not suspected of any wrongdoing.*[28]

However, collateral intrusion is intrusion upon those who are irrelevant to an investigation. The avoidance of collateral harm will

protect only a subcategory of those who are not suspected of criminal conduct and does not entail special consideration of the relevant
innocent, or of disproportionate harms imposed upon the minimally
responsible.

4.2 Might there be informal sensitivity to liability?

It might be objected that our existing structures do in fact take
account of target responsibility in an oblique way. Thus, it may
be argued that police and security service practices are appropriately morally sensitive, even if the laws do not expressly demand
that they do so. Perhaps the correct spirit in interpreting laws
and policies is to take a charitable approach that includes the
injection of the right normative position where it is possible and
appropriate to do so, and that the inclusion of considerations of
perceived responsibility for wrongdoing in judgments of proportionality is a perfect example of this. In the philosophical
literature, several specifically argue against a consequentialist
interpretation of proportionality.[29] And in the legal literature it
is sometimes argued that proportionality is a rich concept that is
liable to several different interpretations, and further that some
of these interpretations permit the inclusion of wider moral concepts of the kind that I am describing, such as the target's responsibility for wrongdoing.[30]

However, it is striking that the governance structure calls attention
to a series of specific factors in considering proportionality (crime,
national security, degree of intrusion, collateral intrusion), but does
not include in the factors to be considered the degree of perceived
involvement or responsibility of those targeted. Especially where
operations are not approved by judges, it would be optimistic to rely
upon such a jurisprudential or philosophical subtlety in arguing that
the current governance structure is effective in implementing the
ethical concept of proportionality that I describe here. In short, we
would do better to legislate our values directly. We are currently in
the unstable situation in which a rule that does not exist is widely
assumed into existence merely by virtue of its plausibility. Insofar as
our values are being enacted anyhow, then regulatory change would
be relatively costless and would have the benefit of ensuring that
those values continue to be honoured.

The approach that I have sketched out makes a clear distinction between those who are merely of intelligence interest and those who are of intelligence interest because they are believed to be involved in wrongdoing. One may speculate that that distinction is commonly elided partly as a result of a tendency to assume that those who are of intelligence interest *are* in some way up to no good; in other words, we 'other' the criminal class, so that from a privileged position it is assumed that such intrusions will never happen to *us*. Of course, once stated, the fallacy of this position becomes self-evident. This is compatible with it being present in, and indeed corrupting of, our public discourse.[31] A tendency to conflate intelligence-worthiness with culpability, to assume implicitly that where there is smoke there is fire, distracts us from a proper account of the proportionality of state intrusions.

A second reason to conflate intelligence-worthiness with culpability is perhaps a tendency to focus on the simple case, in which an individual is involved in wrongdoing and is surveilled. Such a tendency has arguably become less pervasive since the increase in intelligence-led policing and surveillance; it is now hard to imagine, for example, a leader claiming that surveillance will not apply to 'ordinary people' because they are not of interest.

Third, it may be the case that the non-culpable intelligence-worthy target has hitherto been a comparatively small category, encouraging an ongoing focus upon the simple case. In short, police are normally involved with criminals. The property of being a useful target will tend to track the property of being believed to be culpable. Even if the rules governing the use of covert police do not legislate for sensitivity to perceived responsibility or culpability, there are, none-theless, straightforward criminological facts and institutional pressures or habits that render it likely that the rules are applied in a way that respond to target's mode of agency. Gray argues, 'Because it is expensive, most of us can be secure that we are not, never have been, and never will be subject to extended human surveillance, whether reasonable or not'.[32] Put bluntly, police are typically involved with criminals. The crime level is high, in comparison to the levels of resources that are made to combat it. Covert policing and surveil-lance – along with the corresponding analysis of the information it produces – are relatively expensive strategies. The natural way to deploy these resources is to use them against those who are strongly suspected of committing crimes. In this context, where suspicion is plentiful in comparison to the resources that might be deployed to meet it, it would be wasteful to use policing resources anywhere else. Perhaps, continues the argument, there is a possible world in which the ratio of crime-to-crime-prevention resources is different. In that world, it becomes efficient for crime-prevention purposes to use covert methods often on those against whom there is no reasonable suspicion. This may be the kind of nightmare described in genuine totalitarian dystopias, or police states, where neighbours act as informants upon one another. But as things are, it looks to the analyst that the marginal security benefit of focusing resources on those against whom there is strong suspicion of criminal activity is almost always higher than that which arises when focusing on those against whom there is not strong suspicion. Thus, in practice, it might be argued that we have, in effect, what I am calling a culpability model, even if its governance appears to be efficacy-focused.

Fourth, it may be the case that the distinction between culpability and intelligence-worthiness has thus far mattered less because institutional culture leads to greater intrusions upon those perceived to be more culpable. In short, the tendency to assume that the law *does* respond to culpability permeates into the practices of police and security agencies themselves. Indeed, the law has punched above its weight in institutional terms. RIPA is formally a piece of enabling legislation; although the governance structure 'strongly recommend[s]' (Home Office 2014, s 2.12) that agencies follow it, it expressly provides no sanction where its procedures are not followed, and even declares that it does not 'create a preferential legislative regime' (RIPA s.80). It has therefore been proposed that this 'arguably makes RIPA no more than a voluntary code'.[33] Despite this, a recent series of ethnographic studies shows that RIPA has had a significant effect on limiting the practice of covert policing across the UK and is considered by many officers to be onerous.[34] One may speculate that a reason for this forceful impact is that the requirement to provide a rationale is sufficient to lead those seeking authorisation for covert work to reflect upon proportionality as it is intuitively understood. Even though the legal sense of proportionality only very weakly demands any consideration of culpability, perhaps it is natural for those implementing the rules as they are stated to 'read in' culpability considerations.

However, this does not allay the concern. There are limitations to the aforementioned four points. The first two (that there has been a tendency to 'other' those connected to criminal wrongs, and to focus on the simple case) are based on misconceptions, the third (that police will in fact typically be involved with criminals) is questionable, and in any case all four are likely to become decreasingly true. As the technological landscape alters and as police and security work is increasingly intelligence-focused, the category of the intelligence-worthy innocent target will expand. If the culpability idea is part of our ethical conception of proportionality, then we would do better to implement it in express regulations or codes of practice, rather than to depend upon the empirics to ensure its application. It is in an important sense a matter of serendipity that the current governance model will not in general result in serious intrusions upon known innocents. Whereas the responsibility idea holds that it is *in principle* permissible to engage in a greater intrusion upon those who are involved in a higher degree of harm, the current approach has only as a *likely outcome* that the more malicious will face more intrusions. And there are possible exceptions to the likely facts that currently make it the case that the innocent have de facto extra protections.

The institutional habit of being restrained by and seeking to get authorisation through the legislative framework may also change. Sociological evidence on how the institution of police tends now to behave is an imperfect guide to future behaviour. There is a line of precedents in which the governance structure has not been followed and in which prosecutions have nonetheless succeeded.[35] If this continues, then institutional culture may shift. This point is intensified by the way in which the scope of Court scrutiny itself is limited, especially when contrasted with the broader long-term trend for policing to tilt towards a focus on prevention and intelligence.[36] As this continues, the scrutiny of the courts will cover a smaller part of police activity. The 2012 report on criminality and protest by Her Majesty's Inspectorate of Constabulary offers an instance of this trend in the context of covert work:

> Accountability to the court . . . provides an incentive for police to implement the system of control rigorously: but in HMIC's view, this incentive did not exist for the [National Public Order Intelligence Unit].[37]

The incentives provided to police by the Office of Surveillance Commissioners and the Investigatory Powers Tribunal are weak in comparison to the possibility of the collapse of a trial and direct judicial criticism.[38] Even if police and intelligence agencies are responsive to responsibility judgments now, there are trends that imply they will be less responsive in the future as the enabling aspect of the current governance structure becomes institutionally apparent. And even if there will not be a general trend that counterbalances the seeking of overdeveloped authorisations, we can expect the considerations I have advanced in the last two paragraphs to provide a bulwark of exceptions to the optimistic possibility in which innocents receive special consideration by the good grace of institutional habit.

4.3   Judicial involvement

There are three sources of regulation of an intrusive tactic like undercover policing. First, there are internal authorisations from the police. Second, there is oversight and authorisation from judicial and non-judicial bodies outside of the police. Third, there are the incentives created by the criminal courts, and in particular the rules of evidence in court that would provide a stay of a trial or an exclusion of evidence on the grounds of entrapment.

We have seen that, because it can be useful in intelligence or policing terms to use undercover policing with goals other than the building of a prosecution of the immediate target, it is insufficient to rely on court processes as regulative instruments. The regulations that govern the police manipulation encourage a focus on the courts and post hoc judicial oversight. In the United Kingdom, if the police act unconscionably in causing a crime, then a stay of trial can be argued for. In the United States, entrapment is a defence at trial. Police manipulations have thus traditionally been governed through the criminal courts through the threat of the collapse of a trial. This sits poorly with a policing structure that increasingly has the immediate goal of its activities' outcomes other than successfully prosecuted trials.[39]

The case I have made here suggests a reason in favour of a strong form of judicial involvement. It suggests prior judicial authorisation of the use of intrusive investigative techniques. The reason for this is that, if the ethical structure I have suggested is enacted, then in making judgments of proportionality, it becomes necessary to decide not just matters of external fact – What is the target planning? How much harm might the operation cause? What other methods might be used in dealing with the threat? – but also internal matters relating to intent and responsibility. A target may be less culpable because she has been exploited, or lacks the *mens rea* even for any inchoate crime, or could not reasonably have been expected to have foreseen that her actions would contribute to a harm. Judgments of this kind are paradigmatic of the judiciary's distinctive institutional contribution: it is staffed by people who are trained in evaluations of responsibility, and it has relative independence in an area in which decisions are liable to be swayed. None of the other groups who might be responsible for authorisation – the Secretary of State, an independent body staffed by ex-intelligence officers, senior serving police officers – meet the criteria needed to perform this task of making reliable judgments of responsibility as completely as the judge. Proportionality rightly depends not merely on whether targets have acted or intend to act in some harmful way and on what the effects of the intrusion would be on them and third parties, but also on whether the target has a culpable state of mind, or has excuses. With the premise that the judiciary is in a position to properly fulfil this function, we have a strong reason in favour of judicial authorisation.

Existing structures in the UK only demand prior external authorisation in the case of long-term deployments; otherwise, approval is obtained from senior officers. Several have noted that there is a discrepancy between the relatively low level of authority that is needed in order to authorise an undercover operation, and the high level of authority that is needed to authorise surveillance and searches.[40] Warrants for interceptions of communications need to be signed by the Home Secretary. Judges issue search warrants. Involvement with covert police arguably opens up an individual to greater intrusions, since targets can be manipulated and not merely surveilled.[41] Aside from influencing behaviour, 'human bugs' can ask leading questions, whereas mechanical bugs are passive. Undercover agents can gain access to a house without a warrant, in a procedure that skirts the spirit of the need for judge-approved warrants for house searches. The situation appears to be inconsistent and would be resolved with prior judicial authorisation of undercover policing.

5 Concluding note

In this book I have argued that the central distinction in understanding the ethics of undercover policing is the idea of liability. This idea gives us insight into how to see undercover policing as proportionate or disproportionate. Taking account not just of the harms and benefits of an operation, but also of the perceived involvement in wrongdoing of those who are affected, leads us towards a framework for understanding undercover policing ethics that is more in line with our values. In Chapters 1 and 2, I explored the forms of undercover policing and the ways it may be justified, emphasising the way in which I am putting forward an argument in the realm of ideals. Chapters 3 and 4 laid out and defended the liability framework. Chapter 5 applied the framework to the issue of police manipulation, using this as a lens through which to examine stings and entrapment. Finally, in this chapter, I have set out some governance structures that are suggested by the liability framework that I have defended in the book. In particular, I have argued that 'otherwise illegal activity' can be authorised with close oversight; that there should be a central body that governs undercover policing; and that there are strong reasons for judicial oversight.

Notes

1 'The Spycops Bill Undermines the Rule of Law and Gives a Green Light to Serious Crimes | Shami Chakrabarti', 14 October 2020. www.theguardian.com/commentisfree/2020/oct/14/spycops-bill-undermines-rule-of-law-green-light-serious-crimes-undercover-officers.
2 Hunt, Luke William. The Retrieval of Liberalism in Policing. Oxford: Oxford University Press, 2018.
3 Ibid.
4 He states: "by sting operations I mean undercover operations in which law enforcement officers – and [informants] – gather evidence against criminal subjects by engaging in clandestine acts that would otherwise be a violation of substantive criminal law". Apart from being narrow in including otherwise illegal activity within it, this definition is also broad in that it seems to include otherwise illegal infiltration that does not seek to procure any act from the target or create any opportunity for criminality. For example, an officer might use a false certificate of a degree in order to gain employment at the target's workplace, in order to spy on her. This is a sting, in Hunt's terms. Here, we would call this observation and infiltration. In any case, it is worth examining the values around all of these types of undercover work.

5 Serious Crime Act 2007. Sections 44–46.

6 Ibid.

7 Fuller, L. 'Positivism and Fidelity to Law: A Reply to Hart'. Harvard Law Review 71, no. 4 (1958): 630–72.

8 Raz, Joseph. The Authority of Law: Essays on Law and Morality. Reprinted. Oxford: Oxford University Press, 2002, p. 211.

9 Waldron, Jeremy. The Rule of Law and the Measure of Property. Cambridge: Cambridge University Press, 2012, pp. 47ff.

10 Ibid., pp. 217–18.

11 Bindman, Jacob. The Covert Human Intelligence Sources (Criminal Conduct) Bill, 2020. www.gardencourtchambers.co.uk/news/the-covert-human-intelligence-sources-criminal-conduct-bill-2020 (accessed May 2021).

12 Walker, Clive. 'Counterterrorism within the Rule of Law? Rhetoric and Reality with Special Reference to the United Kingdom'. Terrorism and Political Violence 33, no. 2 (17 February 2021): 338–52, 342. Quoting Reprieve and others, Briefing for Second Reading of the Covert Human Intelligence Sources (Criminal Conduct) Bill (London: 2020), 1.

13 Ibid.

14 Joh, Elizabeth E. 'Breaking the Law to Enforce It: Undercover Police Participation in Crime'. Stanford Law Review 62, no. 1 (2009): 183.

15 Joh, Elizabeth E., and Thomas Wuil Joo. 'Sting Victims: Third-Party Harms in Undercover Police Operations'. Southern California Law Review 88 (2015): 1311.

16 E.g., Penney, Jonathon W. 'Chilling Effects: Online Surveillance and Wikipedia Use'. Berkeley Technology Law Journal 31, no. 1 (2016): 117–82.

17 Skolnick, Jerome H. 'Deception by Police'. Criminal Justice Ethics 1, no. 2 (1982): 45.

18 Ibid., p. 52.

19 Skolnick asserts that the hypothesis "cannot be tested", since "a true test would require an experimental design where we could manipulate the independent variable (authoritative permission to employ investigative trickery) and measure the dependent variable (courtroom perjury by police). Since we can neither manipulate the former nor measure the latter, the hypothesis, however plausible, must remain speculative." Ibid., p. 45. There are, however, in principle, ways of testing the hypothesis. We might, for example, compare jurisdictions in which police have different degrees of permission to dissemble at the investigative stage, and measure courtroom perjury through the use of anonymous surveys.

20 Ibid., p. 42.

21 Loftus, Bethan, Benjamin Goold, and Shane Mac Giollabhui. 'From a Visible Spectacle to an Invisible Presence: The Working Culture of Covert Policing'. British Journal of Criminology 56, no. 4 (2016): 629–45.

22 R v Barkshire and others [2011] EWCA Crim 1885; Lewis, Paul, and Rob Evans. Undercover: The True Story of Britain's Secret Police. London: Guardian Faber Publishing, 2014.

23 Harfield, Clive. 'Undercover Policing: A Legal-Comparative Perspective'. In Comparative Policing from a Legal Perspective, edited by Monica den Boer. Cheltenham: Edward Elgar Publishing, 2018, pp. 153–68. See also Ross, Jacqueline E. 'Impediments to Transnational Cooperation in Undercover Policing: A Comparative Study of the United States and Italy'. The American Journal of Comparative Law 52, no. 3 (2004).

24 The Regulation of Investigatory Powers Act 2000 (RIPA) makes this specification for each of the powers it confers. Depending on the particular power these purposes include: national security, preventing or detecting serious crime, the economic well-being of the nation, public safety, public health, collecting tax, preventing death or injury, investigating miscarriages of justice, identifying the deceased, regulating financial markets. See RIPA ss. 28(3) and 29(3).

25 Taylor, Nick. 'To Find the Needle Do You Need the Whole Haystack? Global Surveillance and Principled Regulation'. The International Journal of Human Rights 18, no. 1 (2 January 2014): 53.

26 August 2018 Revised Code of Practice on Covert Human Intelligence Sources. It is curious that collateral intrusions, and not collateral harms in general, are referred to here. As we have seen, the possibilities of third-party harms in covert investigation go beyond mere intrusions. For example, stings can have serious economic effects on uninvolved parties.

27 Below, I consider and raise doubts about the possibility that perceived responsibility or culpability may be taken into account implicitly.

28 Anderson, David. 'A Question of Trust'. Investigatory Powers Review (June 2015): 251. https://terrorismlegislationreviewer.independent.gov.uk/wp-content/uploads/2015/06/IPR-Report-Print-Version.pdf (accessed May 2021). italics added.

29 Hurka, T. 'Proportionality in the Morality of War'. Philosophy & Public Affairs 33 (2005): 34–66; Macnish, K. 'An Eye for an Eye: Proportionality and Surveillance'. Ethical Theory and Moral Practice 18 (2015): 529–48.

30 For example, Hickman proposes a proportionality test with two elements: the 'overall' and the 'relative' (Hickman, Tom. 'The Substance and Structure of Proportionality'. Public Law 4 (2008): 694–716); see also Huscroft, G., B. W. Miller, and G. Webber, eds. Proportionality and the Rule of Law: Rights, Justification, Reasoning. Cambridge: Cambridge University Press, 2014.

31 Analogously, in the context of gangs and race, folk 'signifiers' can have the effect of legitimising the over-policing of subsets of the population (Williams, Patrick. 'Criminalising the Other: Challenging the Race-Gang Nexus'. Race & Class 56, no. 3 (2015): 18–35).

32 Gray, David. 'A Collective Right to Be Secure from Unreasonable Tracking'. Texas Tech Law Review 48 (2015): 202.

33 McKay, Simon. Covert Policing: Law and Practice. 2nd edition. Oxford: Oxford University Press, 2015, p. 141. RIPA does not directly overrule existing limitations that exist in other parts of the law. It provides a formal process backed by legislation where previously there was none.

34 Giollabhuí, Shane Mac, Benjamin Goold, and Bethan Loftus. 'Watching the Watchers: Conducting Ethnographic Research on Covert Police Investigation in the United Kingdom'. Qualitative Research (3 February 2016).

35 Walker, C., and K. Hyland. 'Undercover Policing and Underwhelming Laws'. Criminal Law Review 8 (2014): 555–74.

36 Bowling, B., and J. W. E. Sheptycki. Global Policing. Los Angeles: SAGE Publications Ltd, 2011; Innes, M., and J. Sheptycki. 'From Detection to Disruption: Intelligence and the Changing Logic of Police Crime Control in the United Kingdom'. International Criminal Justice Review 14 (2004); Marx, G. T. 'Who Really Gets Stung? Some Issues Raised by the New Police Undercover Work'. Crime & Delinquency 28 (1982): 166–7.

37 HMIC. 'A Review of National Police Units Which Provide Intelligence on Criminality Associated with Protest'. 2012, p. 7. www.justiceinspectorates.gov.uk/hmicfrs/publications/review-of-national-police-units-which-provide-intelligence-on-criminality-associated-with-protest-20120202/ (accessed May 2021).

38 Harfield, C. The Governance of Covert Investigation. Melbourne University Law Review 34 (2010): 773.

39 Davies, Gemma. 'Shining a Light on Policing of the Dark Web: An Analysis of UK Investigatory Powers'. The Journal of Criminal Law 84, no. 5 (1 October 2020): 407–26; Giollabhuí, Shane Mac, Benjamin Goold, and Bethan Loftus, 'Watching the Watchers: Conducting Ethnographic Research on Covert Police Investigation in the United Kingdom'. Qualitative Research 16, no. 6 (2016): 630–45.

40 Harfield, C. 'The Governance of Covert Investigation'. Melbourne University Law Review 34 (2010): 773; Jerome, H. Skolnick. 'Deception By Police'. Criminal Justice Ethics 1, no. 40 (1982); Walker, C., and K. Hyland. 'Undercover Policing and Underwhelming Laws'. Criminal Law Review 8 (2014): 555–74.

41 Kleinig, John. The Ethics of Policing. Cambridge: Cambridge University Press, 1996, pp. 135–6.

Index

Note: names are only listed in the index where they are used in the main text of book.

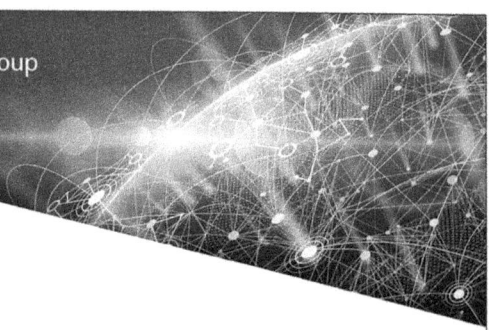

For Product Safety Concerns and Information please contact our EU
representative GPSR@taylorandfrancis.com
Taylor & Francis Verlag GmbH, Kaufingerstraße 24, 80331 München, Germany

www.ingramcontent.com/pod-product-compliance
Lightning Source LLC
Chambersburg PA
CBHW061750270326
41928CB00011B/2449